MY ANCESTOR WAS SCOTTISH

by Alan Stewart

SOCIETY OF GENEALOGISTS ENTERPRISES LTD.

Published by
Society of Genealogists Enterprises Limited
14 Charterhouse Buildings, Goswell Road
London EC1M 7BA.

ISBN: 978-1-907199-13-4

British Library Cataloguing in Publication Data.
A CIP Catalogue record for this book is available from the British Library.

The Society of Genealogists Enterprises Limited is a wholly owned subsidiary of the Society of Genealogists, a registered charity, no 233701.

About the Author

Alan Stewart is a former information technology manager who has been tracing his own ancestors for over 30 years. During all of this time he has been a member of the Society of Genealogists (SoG). Alan has been published in the *Financial Times* and *Encyclopedia Britannica*, writes for several family history magazines (both in the United Kingdom and in North America), gives talks at the SoG library in London, and is a member of the User Group for the ScotlandsPeople website. This is Alan's fourth published book, and his third on family history.

Cover Images - Foreground: *Campbell of Argyle*. A romanticised Victorian-era illustration of a Clansman by R. R. McIan from *The Clans of the Scottish Highlands* published in 1845. Cityscape: Castle Street and municipal buildings, Aberdeen, Scotland, between 1890 and 1905. Inset: The signet of Bishop Jocelin of Glasgow, 1843. Background: Map of the clans of Scotland with the possessions of the Highland Proprietors according to the Acts of Parliament of 1587 & 1594. Published 1899. Public domain images.

CONTENTS

List of illustrations

CHAPTER ONE
Introduction

Researching ancestry has never been more popular with more and more books, magazines, websites and databases becoming available every day and television programmes reflecting and encouraging this interest. The sheer amount of information available can be overwhelming, which means there is still a need for a concise, clear guide to help you get started.

Living in the South of England, and as an experienced writer and teacher of Scottish genealogy to a largely English audience, it became apparent to me that there was a need for a guide aimed at genealogists who may have some familiarity with records and research south of the border but who need to get to grips with the differences and nuances of researching in Scotland.

Hence I was delighted to accept the Society of Genealogists' express invitation to write such a guide. This book is written for the family historian who perhaps has some understanding of tracing English ancestry but who is not particularly familiar with Scotland and its distinct records, which can in many ways be more informative than those found in England and Wales.

Although the basic techniques of Scottish family history are the same as those for English and Welsh research, there are a number of differences, because Scotland retained its own legal system when its Parliament was

united with England's in 1707. (The two countries have had the same monarch since King James VI of Scotland became James I of England in 1603.)

Tracing your ancestors in Scotland certainly has much in common with family history research in England and Wales: the principal documents you need to consult are civil registration birth, marriage and death records; the 1841-1911 census returns; baptisms, marriages and burials in the parish registers; and wills/testaments. This book, however, will reflect the distinctly Scottish nature of the legal, religious and civil records north of the border.

One distinct advantage for anyone tracing their Scottish ancestors is that all of these records are held pretty much in one place, in Edinburgh, by the National Records of Scotland (NRS), which was formed in April 2011 by the merger of the General Register Office for Scotland (GROS) and the National Archives of Scotland (NAS, formerly the Scottish Record Office).

However, if you can't travel to Scotland, then this book will guide you to alternatives found online and outside Scotland, for example in the Library of the Society of Genealogists in London, or microfilmed by The Church of Jesus Christ of Latter-day Saints and available to view in local Mormon Family History Centres around the country (and indeed around the world).

Civil registration

The information found in certificates of birth, marriage and deaths registered by the State is invaluable to family historians. This began in Scotland on 1 January 1855, rather than 1 July 1837, as in England and Wales. Although beginning later, Scottish birth, marriage and death records contain more information than English and Welsh certificates.

For example, birth records contain the date and place of the parents' marriage; marriage records have not only the fathers' names, but also the mothers' forenames and maiden surnames; and death records give the names of both parents (if known), including the mother's maiden surname. In the first year of civil registration, the records contained even more information. We will look in detail at these records in Chapter 2.

Census returns

Although originally taken for Governments' statistical and administrative purposes, for family historians the records of the census provide a valuable snapshot of detailed information about individuals and families living at a particular address on a particular night. The census was taken every ten years from 1801, and from 1841-1911 the census returns can provide clues and information on ages, relationships and places of births of our ancestors who were alive in the Victorian and Edwardian period.

Luckily, for some years, the Scottish census returns give even more information than the English, such as whether someone could speak Gaelic (in the 1891-1911 censuses) and the number of rooms with windows (given from 1861-1911). There are also several surviving returns from 1801-1831 that list individual names, although (as in England and Wales) this was not officially required. More information about these vital genealogical records can be found in Chapter 3, while Chapter 4 covers other population listings, such as valuation rolls, taxation records and militia lists.

Parish registers

Church records remain the most important genealogical sources for the period before the census years. The Scottish national church is the Church of Scotland, which was supposed to keep records from 1553, although it's rare for there to be registers of a parish church from as early as that.

Only two baptisms (in Errol, Perthshire) were actually recorded in 1553 (and they were in December). Two other parishes later recorded burials that had taken place prior to 1553, however. Generally, parish registers began in the mid-17th century (and in the Highlands and islands in the late 18th and even 19th centuries). Many of the 'marriage' records in the parish registers are actually those of the proclamation of banns.

As the Church of Scotland registers up to 1854 were handed in to the GROS, they are known as the Old Parochial (or Parish) Registers (OPRs). In Scotland, there are no bishops' transcripts of the registers. We will look at the OPRs etc in Chapter 5 and other church records in Chapter 6.

Wills/testaments

Where they exist, wills can supplement what are known as Vital Records (births, baptisms, marriages, deaths and burials) by providing information not only on the property owned and bequeathed to friends and family, but even the wishes and words of testators. As Scotland has its own distinct and venerable legal system, the equivalent of its probate documents, processes and terminology can be unfamiliar to the English ear.

All testaments testamentar (wills) and testaments dative (administrations of estates of those who did not leave wills) were confirmed (proved) in commissary courts from 1513 up to the 1820s and in sheriff courts after that. In Scotland, you will not find mention of the Prerogative or 'peculiar' courts that typified the church courts that dealt with probate matters in England and Wales. Scottish wills/testaments will be looked at in depth in Chapter 7.

Online records

The great advantage for those of us with Scottish ancestry, but who don't live in Scotland - and also for many who do - is that images of all the above record types are available online at the official ScotlandsPeople pay-per-view website **www.scotlandspeople.gov.uk**.

There is a rolling cut-off point for viewing civil registration records on the site of 100 years for births, 75 years for marriages and 50 years for deaths. More recent records (up to 2009) are included in the indexes and can be ordered online for delivery by post.

Census returns are online from 1841-1911, parish registers from 1538 (at the earliest) up to 1854, and wills from 1513-1901 (which is expected to be extended to 1925 shortly).

In addition, ScotlandsPeople has images of Roman Catholic births/baptisms, marriages, deaths/burials and some other records from the 18th to the 20th centuries; and coats of arms records from 1672-1908. Valuation records (covered in Chapter 4) from the 19th and early 20th centuries are being added to the site, and other types of record - such as kirk session (the equivalent of the vestry in England and Wales), criminal court, Poor Law and land records - are expected to be in the future.

There are many other websites that contain family history information specific to individual Scottish counties and other local areas, and these are dealt with in Chapter 15.

Other records

As well as (Presbyterian) Church of Scotland, Roman Catholic and Nonconformist (Baptist, Congregationalist, Methodist, Quaker, etc.) registers, Scotland also has registers of the many (Presbyterian) 'Secession' churches that broke away from the Church of Scotland, mainly in the 18th and 19th centuries (such as the Free Church of Scotland). Chapter 6 deals with this subject.

The National Archives at Kew holds many records that are just as relevant in searching for Scottish ancestors as they are for English and Welsh. Some of these documents are available online, such as the many armed forces records (covered in Chapter 9), as well as passenger lists, both outgoing and incoming.

Also in the book

The remaining chapters of the book will help you to fill in the background of your Scots ancestors, while also looking at local information and some useful Scottish legal records.

Chapter 8 tells you something about the general ancestry of the Scots, the Highland clans and why so many Scotsmen and women are likely to be descended from King Robert the Bruce. Scotland's maps are covered in Chapter 10, while the following chapter looks at Scottish newspapers and where you can find them.

Scotland is very fortunate to have detailed descriptions of each parish, dating back to the late 18th century, and these 'statistical accounts' are covered in Chapter 12. Also unique to Scotland are the inheritance records known as 'services of heirs' or 'retours' (returns) covering the period 1545-1859 (which have led me to parts of my family tree that I would otherwise not have known about). These records are dealt with in Chapter 13.

Scottish legal records are quite different to those of England and Wales, and Chapter 14 looks at both land records ('sasines') and those of the criminal courts. Finally, Scotland's archives and family history societies are looked at in Chapter 17.

Scottish local government

In the 1975 re-organisation of Scottish local government, Scotland's 33 historic counties (containing about 900 ancient parishes) were replaced by 13 regions, which were in turn superseded by 32 unitary authorities in 1996. All references in this book will be to the historic counties.

The library of the Society of Genealogists

At the end of most chapters of this book, I've indicated whether there are record copies or transcriptions in the library of the Society of Genealogists in London. In addition, Chapter 16 lists many other Scottish resources in the library.

Dunnottar Castle, 2007, by Maciej Lewandowski.

CHAPTER TWO
Civil Registration

Scottish civil registration records (or, as they are officially known, the Statutory Registers of Births, Marriages and Deaths) contain more information than their counterparts in England and Wales. Civil registration came to Scotland seventeen and a half years later, but made up for its lateness by providing much more than in similar records south of the border.

This was particularly the case in Scottish civil registration's first year (1855). Unfortunately for us, it was found to be too much of a chore for both the registrars and the public to continue to provide the high quantity of information that was required in the first year. In 1856, a good deal less was contained in the records, with some items restored in 1861.

Birth records

The chart below compares Scottish birth records in 1855, from 1856-1860, and from 1861 onwards, with those of England and Wales:

Information	England & Wales	Scotland 1861 onwards	Scotland 1856-1860	Scotland 1855
When and where born	✓	✓	✓	✓
Hour of birth		✓	✓	✓
Name	✓	✓	✓	✓
Sex	✓	✓	✓	✓
Name and surname of father	✓	✓	✓	✓
Name, surname and maiden name of mother	✓	✓	✓	✓
Occupation of father	✓	✓	✓	✓
Signature, description and residence of informant	✓	✓	✓	✓
When registered	✓	✓	✓	✓
Where registered		✓	✓	✓
Signature of registrar	✓	✓	✓	✓
Name entered after registration	✓		✓	✓
Date and place of (parents') marriage		✓		✓
Baptismal name (if different)				✓
Age of father				✓
Birthplace of father				✓
Issue, living and deceased				✓
Age of mother				✓
Birthplace of mother				✓
Position of child in family (e.g. 5th child)				1

Note 1: The position of the child in the family was not officially asked for.

The date and place of the parents' marriage is very useful in getting back another generation, but the information may not be correct. I came across an instance where the birth record of a couple's first child in 1885 stated that they had married in February 1884 in Glasgow. On their second child's birth record three years later, however, the year of marriage was still 1884, but the month had changed to January and the place to Edinburgh. It's hardly surprising that I couldn't find their marriage in either city!

In my own family, one set of great-grandparents married on 16 June 1884, but their first child had been born exactly a month earlier. On the birth certificates of their next five children, they tried to hide this illegitimacy by specifying 16 May as the date of their marriage, but left the year as 1884. I would have thought this would still have caused some embarrassment when they celebrated the eldest child's birthday and their wedding anniversary on the same day and with the same number of years!

The extra information provided in 1855 is so helpful that, even if you don't have an ancestor who was born in that year, it's good if you can find a sibling who was. Unfortunately, many people in my extended family seem to have been born in either 1854 or 1856!

Marriage records

The chart below compares Scottish marriage records in 1855 and from 1856 onwards, with those of England and Wales:

Information	England & Wales	Scotland 1856 onwards	Scotland 1855
When married	✓	✓	✓
Name and surname	✓	✓	✓
Age	✓	✓	✓
Condition (marital status)	✓	✓	✓
Rank or profession	✓	✓	✓
Residence at time of marriage	✓	✓	✓
Father's name and surname	✓	✓	✓
Rank or profession of father	✓	✓	✓
Where married	✓	✓	✓
According to which rites and ceremonies	✓	✓	✓
Signature of registrar or clergyman	✓		
Names and surnames of witnesses	✓	✓	✓
Relationship (if any)		✓	✓
Mother's name and maiden surname		✓	✓
When and where registered		✓	✓
For regular marriages - Signature of clergyman		✓	✓
For irregular marriages - Date of Extract Sentence of Conviction or Decree of Declarator, and in what court pronounced		✓	✓
Signature of registrar		✓	✓
Usual address (as well as present address)			✓
Whether 2nd or 3rd marriage (if widowed)			✓
Children by each former marriage, living and dead			✓
Birthplace			✓
When and where birth registered			✓

All Scottish marriage records give the forenames and maiden surnames of the mothers of the bride and groom, as well as their fathers. This is very useful to know when you're looking for the birth record of the bride or groom, so that you can tell whether you've found the right one.

Until 1 July 1940, there were no civil marriages performed by registrars in Scotland. Up to that time, marriages were either regular (performed in church by a clergyman) or irregular (by declaration in the presence of witnesses). Marriages over the anvil at Gretna Green and other places were examples of irregular marriages.

Death records

The chart below compares Scottish death records in 1855, from 1856-1860, and from 1861 onwards, with those of England and Wales:

Information	England & Wales	Scotland 1861 onwards	Scotland 1856-1860	Scotland 1855
When and where died	✓	✓	✓	✓
Name and surname	✓	✓	✓	✓
Sex	✓	✓	✓	✓
Age	✓	✓	✓	✓
Occupation	✓	✓	✓	✓
Cause of death	✓	✓	✓	✓
Signature, description and residence of informant	✓	✓	✓	1
When registered	✓	✓	✓	✓
Signature of registrar	✓	✓	✓	✓
Whether single, married or widowed	2	✓	✓	
Name and surname of father		✓	✓	✓
Rank and profession of father		✓	✓	✓
Name and maiden surname of mother		✓	✓	✓
Duration of disease		✓	✓	✓
Medical attendant by whom certified		✓	✓	✓
Where registered		✓	✓	✓
Hour of death		3	✓	✓
When medical attendant last saw the deceased			✓	✓
Burial place			✓	✓
Undertaker or other person by whom certified			✓	✓
Where born				✓
How long deceased lived in present district				✓
Name of spouse	2	4		✓
Issue, in order of birth, their names and ages				5

Notes:

1. Although the 1855 death record asks for only the signature of the informant, the relationship to the deceased is usually given too.
2. Although the English/Welsh death record does not ask for information about her marital status or spouse, in the case of a married woman, the name and occupation of her husband are usually given in the space for 'occupation'.
3. Although the hour of death has not been specifically asked for since 1860, it is in fact still given.
4. Similarly, although the name of the deceased's spouse has not been specifically requested since 1855, it has in fact been given again since 1861.
5. Not only are the names and ages given for the children of the marriage, but in the case of those who had already died, their ages at death and year of death are given.

It's very useful to find the names of the deceased person's parents on a death certificate, but the informants didn't always get the names quite right, and sometimes they didn't know them at all.

Register of Corrected Entries

If something had to be added to or corrected on a birth, marriage or death entry, then the change would be put in the Register of Corrected Entries (RCE, since 1965 standing for the Register of Corrections, Etc.) rather than alter the original record, which would be annotated in the left-hand margin with 'RCE' or 'Reg. Cor. Ent.' plus the volume number, page number and date. For example, one of my ancestors committed suicide and this is indicated on an RCE entry for his death record.

Minor records

The records of births, marriages and deaths of Scottish people outside Scotland are known as the minor records and consist of:

Type of record	Births	Marriages	Deaths
Air Register (1948 onwards)	✓		✓
Consular Returns (1914 onwards)	✓		✓
Foreign Returns (1860-1965)	✓	✓	✓
High Commission Returns (1964 onwards)	✓		✓
Marine Register (1855 onwards)	✓		✓
Service Returns (1881 onwards)	✓	✓	✓
War Returns - South African (Boer) War			✓
War Returns - World War I			✓
War Returns - World War II			✓

ScotlandsPeople

At the official ScotlandsPeople pay-per-view website **www.scotlandspeople.gov.uk**, you can view and download images of the Scottish civil registration (and many other) records. There's a cut-off point for accessing records online of 100 years for births, 75 years for marriages and 50 years for deaths, and that point moves forward a year each January. This means that, at the time of writing (March 2012), you can view and download births up to the end of 1911, marriages to the end of 1936 and deaths to the end of 1961.

ScotlandsPeople uses a credit-based system, under which you can buy 30 credits for £7, having first registered with the website. Searching the indexes is free of charge, but viewing a page of up to 25 results costs one credit and viewing an image costs five credits. If there is an RCE entry for a record, this is flagged up on ScotlandsPeople and you can view the entry at a charge of two credits. The credits are valid for a year and any that you haven't used by the time they expire are added to credits that you buy in the future.

So, for your £7, you can view up to five images, which makes the cost of each record just £1.40. If you have to do more searching before you find a record you want to view, the relative cost of an image will be more, but it'll still be much cheaper (and so much faster) than having to send for a certificate for delivery by post.

However, if you want a birth, marriage or death record (including any of the minor records) that's more recent than 1911, 1936 or 1961 respectively, then you *will* have to order a certificate (unless you make a personal visit to the ScotlandsPeople Centre in Edinburgh). For records up to 2009, you can do this online at ScotlandsPeople, as the statutory birth, marriage and death indexes extend right up to the end of that year. Ordering a certificate online will cost you £12.

You'll also find the Scottish civil registration birth and marriage records from 1855-1875 in the Scottish databases at the FamilySearch website **https://www.familysearch.org** of The Church of Jesus Christ of Latter-day Saints (the 'Mormons').

In the library of the Society of Genealogists

You can search the indexes to the statutory registers of births, marriages and deaths from 1855-1920 on microfilm at the Society of Genealogists' Library, which also holds a microfilm copy of the actual registers themselves for the year 1855.

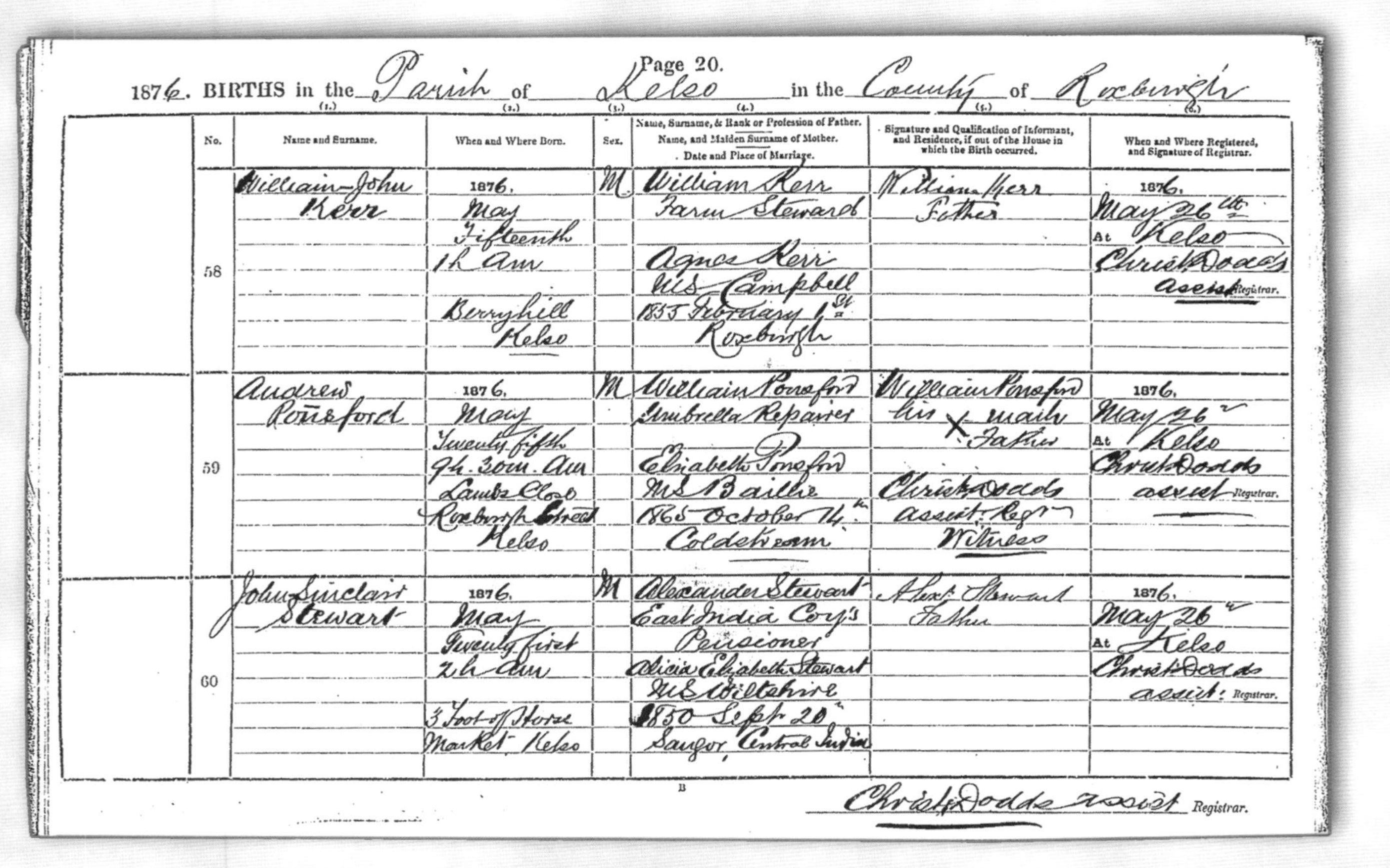

Page 20.

1876. BIRTHS in the Parish of Kelso in the County of Roxburgh

No.	Name and Surname.	When and Where Born.	Sex.	Name, Surname, & Rank or Profession of Father. Name, and Maiden Surname of Mother. Date and Place of Marriage.	Signature and Qualification of Informant, and Residence, if out of the House in which the Birth occurred.	When and Where Registered, and Signature of Registrar.
58	William John Kerr	1876. May Fifteenth 1h Am Berryhill Kelso	M	William Kerr Farm Steward Agnes Kerr M.S. Campbell 1855 February 1st Roxburgh	William Kerr Father	1876. May 26th At Kelso Christ. Dodds assist Registrar.
59	Andrew Ponsford	1876. May Twenty fifth 9h. 30m. Am Lambs Close Roxburgh Street Kelso	M	William Ponsford Umbrella Repairer Elizabeth Ponsford M.S. Baillie 1865 October 14th Coldstream	William Ponsford his X mark Father Christr Dodds assist. Regr Witness	1876. May 26th At Kelso Christ. Dodds assist Registrar.
60	John Sinclair Stewart	1876. May Twenty first 2h Am 3 Foot of Horse Market Kelso	M	Alexander Stewart East India Corp's Pensioner Alicia Elizabeth Stewart M.S. Wiltshire 1850 Sept 20th Saugor, Central India	Alexr Stewart Father	1876. May 26th At Kelso Christ. Dodds assist: Registrar.

B

Christr Dodds assist Registrar.

1. Civil registration births registered in 1876 in Kelso, Roxburghshire.

1880. MARRIAGES in the District of Saint Giles in the City of Edinburgh

(Page 162.)

No.	When, Where, and How Married.	Signatures of Parties. Rank or Profession, whether Single or Widowed, and Relationship (if any).	Age.	Usual Residence.	Name, Surname, and Rank or Profession of Father. Name, and Maiden Surname of Mother.	If a regular Marriage, Signatures of officiating Minister and Witnesses. If irregular, Date of Conviction, Decree of Declarator, or Sheriff's Warrant.	When & Where Registered, and Signature of Registrar.
323	1880. on the Tenth day of December at No 13 St Patrick Square Edinburgh	(Signed) Peter Macgregor Police Constable Bachelor	26	No 13 St Patrick Square Edinburgh	John Macgregor Shepherd deceased and Margaret Macgregor M.S. Cameron (also deceased)	(Signed) John Kay Minister	1880. December 11th At Edinburgh
	After Publication according to the Forms of the U.P. Church	(Signed) Mary Dawson Domestic Servant Spinster	24	No 13 Minto Street Edinburgh	John Dawson Agricultural Labourer and Mary Dawson M.S. Cameron	(Signed) T. Cameron Witness Jessie Dawson Witness	Wm Sutherland Asst Registrar.
324	1880. on the Ninth day of December at Methodist Chapel Victoria Terrace Edinburgh	(Signed) James Smith Butcher (Master) Bachelor	26	No 1 Allan's Close High Street Edinburgh	James Smith Engine Keeper and Catherine Smith M.S. Ross	(Signed) Theophilus Parr	1880. December 10th At Edinburgh
	After Banns according to the Forms of the Methodist Church.	(Signed) Elizabeth Mackintosh Little Spinster	21	No 12 Fells Close Cowgate Edinburgh	Andrew Little Brassfounder's Labourer and St Clair Little M.S. McLeod	(Signed) Fletcher Little Witness B. Campbell Witness	Wm Sutherland Asst Registrar.
	(1.)	(2.)	(3.)	(4.)	(5.)	(6.)	(7.)

M.

Thomas Temple Registrar.

2. Civil registration marriages registered in 1880 in Edinburgh.

—Page 75.—

1903. DEATHS in the District of St. Machar in the Burgh of Aberdeen.

No.	(1.) Name and Surname. Rank or Profession, and whether Single, Married, or Widowed.	(2.) When and Where Died.	(3.) Sex.	(4.) Age.	(5.) Name, Surname, & Rank or Profession of Father. Name, and Maiden Surname of Mother.	(6.) Cause of Death, Duration of Disease, and Medical Attendant by whom certified.	(7.) Signature & Qualification of Informant, and Residence, if out of the House in which the Death occurred.	(8.) When and where Registered, and Signature of Registrar.
223	Mary Williams Keith (Widow of Alexander Keith, Grain Merchant)	1903. February Twenty first 0h. 37m. A.M. 10 Rubislaw Den North, Aberdeen.	F	64 years	Charles Gordon Cooper and Provision Curer (deceased) Ann Gordon M.S. Williams (deceased)	Pleuritis- 8 Days. Pneumonia- 2 Days. As cert. by J.C. Ogilvie Will M.D.	John Henderson Brother-in-law and Occupier (Present.)	1903. February 23rd At Aberdeen James Alston Registrar.
224	Charles Gauld Reid (Single.)	1903. February Twenty second 7h. 30m. P.M. 19 Wallfield Place, Aberdeen	M	17 Months	William Reid Joiner, (Journeyman) Jeannie Reid M.S. Booth	Laryngismus Stridulus.. Asphyxia- 1 Day. As cert. by D. Watson Geddie M.B.	William Reid Father (Present.)	1903. February 23rd At Aberdeen James Alston Registrar.
225	Alexander Peters Stonecutter (Journeyman) (Married to Mary Begg.)	1903. February Twenty first 5h. 20m. P.M. 2 Craigie Loaning Aberdeen	M	45 years	Alexander Peters Road Contractor (deceased) Elspet Peters M.S. Davidson (deceased)	Phthisis- 7 Months. As cert. by James Sinclair M.B.	Annie S. Peters Daughter and Inmate (Present)	1903. February 23rd At Aberdeen James Alston Registrar.

D

James Alston, Registrar.

3. Civil registration deaths registered in 1903 in Aberdeen.

CHAPTER THREE

Censuses

Scottish census returns are very similar to those of England and Wales, beginning in 1801, but without individual names until 1841. As is the case south of the border, there are some lists of names compiled for the 1801-1831 censuses that are still in existence.

The census returns up to 1911 are open to the public, while those from 1921 onwards are not (including the Scottish 1931 census, which still exists, unlike that for England and Wales, which was destroyed in 1940).

The censuses took place on the following dates, showing the population of Scotland to be:

1801	10 March	1,608,420
1811	27 May	1,805,864
1821	28 May	2,091,521
1831	29 May	2,364,386
1841	6 June	2,620,184
1851	30 March	2,888,742
1861	7 April	3,062,294
1871	2 April	3,360,018
1881	3 April	3,735,573
1891	5 April	4,025,647
1901	31 March	4,472,103
1911	2 April	4,759,445

By 1971, Scotland's population had reached a peak of 5,235,600, from which it has dropped to 5,062,011 in 2001. This was estimated to have risen to 5,222,100 in mid-2010, but is expected to remain around that number for the next 20 years.

1841 census

Similarly to the Anglo-Welsh 1841 census, the Scottish version doesn't list exact places of birth. The Scottish census asks 'if born in Scotland, state whether in county or otherwise' or 'whether foreigner, or whether born in England or Ireland'.

In addition, the 1841 census doesn't ask about relationships. However, when searching for my 3x great-grandparents James and Catherine Ross (nee Miller), I found them in the parish of Banchory Ternan in Kincardineshire in 1841 listed as 'James Ross' and 'Catherine Miller (wife)'. On the two pages shown on that image, there are altogether six women listed as 'wife', half of them under their maiden surnames.

The full content in the 1841 census is:

Information	England	Scotland
Place	✓	✓
Houses - uninhabited or building	✓	✓
Houses - inhabited	✓	✓
Names of each person who abode therein the preceding night	✓	✓
Age	✓	✓
Sex	✓	✓
Profession, trade, employment or of independent means	✓	✓
Whether born in same county	✓	✓
Whether born in Scotland, Ireland or foreign parts	✓	
Whether foreigner or whether born in England or Ireland		✓

1851-1911 censuses

As in England and Wales, more questions were added to the census questionnaire over the years, including some that were peculiar to Scotland. From 1861, there was a question on the number of rooms with windows, and from 1891, on whether individuals could speak Gaelic or Gaelic & English. In addition, the 1861 and 1871 censuses asked the number of children between five and 15 years old who were attending school, with the latter census asking about those educated at home.

While researching my great-great-grandfather Robert Munro, I found his family in 1881 living in the parish of Latheron, Caithness. That year, the enumerators had been asked to carry out a trial run to find out the number of Gaelic speakers, although the 1881 census has no question about Gaelic. The enumerator has put '(G)' for the Munro family after 'where born', and this ties in with the family's entries on the 1891 census.

The information given in the censuses from 1851 onwards is:

Information	1851	1861	1871	1881	1891	1901	1911	Scotland only
Schedule number	✓	✓	✓	✓	✓	✓	✓	
Name of street, place or road, and name or number of house	✓	✓	✓	✓	✓	✓	✓	
Houses - uninhabited or building		✓	✓	✓	✓	✓	✓	
Houses - inhabited		✓	✓	✓	✓	✓	✓	
Name and surname of each person who abode in the house	✓	✓	✓	✓	✓	✓	✓	
Number of persons in house							✓	
Relation to head of family	✓	✓	✓	✓	✓	✓	✓	
Condition (marital)	✓	✓	✓	✓	✓	✓	✓	
Age	✓	✓	✓	✓	✓	✓	✓	
Sex	✓	✓	✓	✓	✓	✓	✓	
Duration of marriage							✓	
Children born alive							✓	
Children still living							✓	
Rank, profession or occupation	✓	✓	✓	✓	✓	✓	✓	
Industry or service							✓	
Employer					✓	✓	✓	
Employed					✓	✓	✓	
Working on own account					✓	✓	✓	
Working at home						✓	✓	
Where born	✓	✓	✓	✓	✓	✓	✓	
Nationality if born in a foreign country							✓	
Gaelic or English					✓	✓	✓	1
Whether blind, or deaf and dumb	✓	✓	✓	✓	✓	✓	✓	
Or imbecile or idiot			✓	✓	✓	✓	✓	
Or lunatic			✓	✓	✓	✓	✓	
Number of children from 5-15 attending school		✓	✓					✓
Or being educated at home			✓					✓
Number of rooms with one or more windows		✓	✓	✓	✓	✓	✓	2

Notes:

1. An equivalent question about the ability to speak Welsh was asked in Welsh enumeration districts, which included border areas of England.
2. A question on the number of rooms occupied if less than five was asked in England and Wales in 1891 and 1901.

Censuses online and outside Scotland

You can find images of the 1841-1911 censuses of Scotland at the pay-per-view ScotlandsPeople website **www.scotlandspeople.gov.uk**. In addition, the subscription site Ancestry.co.uk **www.ancestry.co.uk** and the subscription/pay-per-view site Findmypast **www.findmypast.co.uk** have indexed transcriptions of the Scottish 1841-1901 censuses, but neither site has images of the census returns.

Copies of original Scottish census returns can be found on microfilm outside Scotland. Films are available through The Church of Jesus Christ of Latter-day Saints and can be ordered to view at local Mormon Family History Centres. The Society of Genealogists also holds many films of original returns. A few local family history societies have, over the years, transcribed and published the returns for their areas - mostly for the 1851 census. Many of these publications can be found locally or in the library of the Society of Genealogists.

Many volunteers have contributed their work to FreeCEN, the Free Census project, which has also transcribed the 1841-1871 Scottish censuses for some counties. You can view its transcriptions free of charge at the FreeCEN website **www.freecen.org.uk**. Almost all of the 33 historic Scottish counties (and Scottish Shipping for 1861 and 1871) had been at least partially transcribed at the time of writing (March 2012):

- Aberdeenshire (1841, *1851*)
- Angus (1841)
- Argyll (1841, *1851*)
- Ayrshire (1841, 1851)
- Banffshire (1841, 1851, 1861)
- Bute (1841, 1851, 1861, 1871)
- Caithness (1841, 1851, 1861, 1871, *1881*)
- Clackmannanshire (1841)
- Dumfriesshire (1841)
- Dunbartonshire (1841, 1851)
- East Lothian (1841, 1851, 1861)

- Fife (1841, *1851*)
- Inverness-shire (1841, *1851*)
- Kincardineshire (1841, 1851)
- Kinross-shire (1841)
- Kirkcudbrightshire (*1841*)
- Lanarkshire (*1841*, *1851*)
- Midlothian (1841, 1851)
- Moray (1841, 1851, *1861*, *1871*)
- Nairnshire (1841, 1851, *1861*, *1871*)
- Orkney (1841, *1851*)
- Peeblesshire (1841, 1851, 1861, 1871)
- Perthshire (*1841*)
- Renfrewshire (*1841*, *1851*)
- Ross & Cromarty (1841, *1851*)
- Roxburghshire (1841, 1851, *1861*)
- Scottish shipping (*1861*, *1871*)
- Selkirkshire (1841, 1851, 1861, 1871)
- Stirlingshire (1841, 1851)
- Sutherland (*1841*)
- Wigtownshire (1841, 1851, *1861*)
- West Lothian (1841)

For the years shown in italics, the counties are only partially transcribed. FreeCEN has so far carried out no transcriptions at all for Berwickshire or Shetland.

The Friends of the Archives of Dumfries & Galloway have transcribed a number of the Archives' record collections. Among the transcriptions are the 1851 census returns of Dumfriesshire, Kirkcudbrightshire and Wigtownshire, which you can find at the free Historical Indexes micro-site **www.dgcommunity.net/historicalindexes/default.aspx**.

At Graham Maxwell Ancestry **www.maxwellancestry.com/census/default.htm**, you can view free transcriptions of the 1841, 1851 and 1861 censuses of Berwickshire, Peeblesshire, Roxburghshire and Selkirkshire, plus parts of Dumfriesshire (all of the county for 1851), East Lothian and Midlothian. In addition, parts of Kirkcudbrightshire, Lanarkshire and Wigtownshire are available for 1851.

Censuses before 1841 and other population listings

In 1755, Dr. Alexander Webster, Moderator of the General Assembly of the Church of Scotland, had a census carried out by the ministers of all the parishes in Scotland for statistical purposes to assess the size of the population, the results of which (giving no names) you can read and download at the GROS website **www.gro-scotland.gov.uk/files2/the-census/Webster_final.pdf.**

Other pre-1841 censuses that are available online (naming heads of households) include the 1801 census of the parish of Stow, Midlothian, which you can view as part of a subscription to the Statistical Accounts of Scotland **http://edina.ac.uk/stat-acc-scot** (see Chapter 12).

The 1801 census of Dundee is available in transcription at the website of the Friends of Dundee City Archives **www.fdca.org.uk/FDCABurghRecords1.html**.

A transcription of the 1811 census of the parishes of Assynt and Golspie, Sutherland (plus other population lists) is available at Christine Stokes' County Sutherland website **www.countysutherland.co.uk/43.html**.

There are a number of other early censuses and other population lists, most of which are held by the National Records of Scotland. The website of the ScotlandsPeople Centre has a downloadable information leaflet on surviving pre-1841 census listings at **www.scotlandspeoplehub.gov.uk/pdf/pre-1841-census-records.pdf**.

Colin Chapman's book *Pre-1841 Censuses & Population Listings* has information on six surviving parish listings of the census of Scotland for 1801 (three of which list all inhabitants), ten for 1811 (four listing all names), 24 for 1821 (13 listing all names) and ten for 1831 (none of which lists all names).

Chapman also mentions 1695 Poll Tax listings, for Aberdeenshire and Renfrewshire in particular. *Local Census Listings 1522-1930* by Jeremy Gibson and Mervyn Medlycott lists many other local population listings for 22 counties. Gordon Johnson's *Census Records for Scottish Families at Home and Abroad* describes many of these listings in detail.

Directories

You can view (or download for non-commercial use) 694 Post Office Directories from all over Scotland free of charge at the National Library of Scotland's website **www.nls.uk/family-history/directories/post-office**. The directories cover the period 1773-1911.

Directories are helpful for finding ancestors (particularly in towns) in the period before the 1841 census. There are, for example, 44 Glasgow directories at the NLS website covering the period 1783/84 to 1840/41. It can also be useful to refer to directories for the years between censuses, when their entries can help you find when your ancestors changed address.

One drawback to directories is that they tend to list only business- and trades-people and 'the gentry': the earlier volumes list them in alphabetical order, but later ones also list people by street, as well as by occupation. Directories also contain a good deal of other interesting information.

In the library of the Society of Genealogists

In addition to many copies of census returns on film (mentioned above), the library has some published census indexes, particularly for the year 1851. The 1801-1821 censuses of Annan, Dumfriesshire (plus a 1798 tax assessment) have been published in a volume by the Scottish Record Society, a copy of which is held in the Society's library. A search in the Society of Genealogists' free online catalogue shows some 240 entries for Scottish directories held in the SoG's Library. Many of these will also be found on microfilm through local LDS family history centres.

21

Civil Parish and Parish Ward of	Ecclesiastical Parish ~~or Quoad Sacra Parish of~~	School Board District of
Glasgow; Howrth	Barony	Glasgow
Burgh Ward of: Townhead	~~Special Water District of~~	~~Special Drainage District of~~

No. of Schedule. (a)	ROAD, STREET, &c., and No. or NAME of HOUSE. (b)	HOUSES. Inhabited. (c)	HOUSES. Uninhabited (U.), or Building (B.) (d)	Rooms with one or more Windows. (e)	NAME and SURNAME of each Person. (f)	Number of Persons in House. (g)	RELATION to Head of Family. (h)	AGE (last Birthday) and Sex. Males. (i)	AGE (last Birthday) and Sex. Females. (k)	Gaelic or G. & E. (l)	Single, Married, Widower, or Widow. (m)	Married Women. Duration of Marriage. (n)	Married Women. Children born Alive. (o)	Married Women. Children still Living. (p)	
	244 Parliamentary Rd				Maggie Gordon		Daur		5		4				1
					Isabella do		Daur		5		4				2
					Adam Edington		Cousin	26			S				3
					Isabella Dykes		Cousin		20		S				4
140	244 do	1		1	Agnes Hendry	2	Head		33		S				5
					Jeanie do		Sister		19		S				6
141	244 do	1		3	William McInnes	10	Head	43			Mar				7
					Jane do		Wife		36		Mar	18	8	8	8
					Henrietta do		Daur		17		S				9
					Hector do		Son	16	~~16~~		S				10
					John do		Son	14	~~14~~						11
					Jane do		Daur		12						12
					William do		Son	9							13
					James do		Son	7							14
					Alexander do		Son	4							15
					Hugh do		Son	1							16
142	244 do	1		2	Jas. Murray Taylor	6	Head	27			Mar				17
					Euphemia do do		Wife		24		Mar	2	1	1	18
					George Nicol do		Son	10 mo							19
					Mary McDonald		Mother-in-law		64	G&E	W				20
					Donald do		Brother	29			S				21
					Alexander Farquharson		Br	27			Mar				22
143	244 do	1		1	Andrew Macpherson	4	Head	28			Mar				23
					Susan do		Wife		29		Mar	5	1	1	24
					Catherine do		Daur		4						25
					Charles Burns		Step Son	11							26
144	244 do	1		2	Robert Thomson	7	Head	37			Mar				27
					Margaret do		Wife		36		Mar	15	5	3	28
					Rebecca do		Daur		14						29
					Alexander do		Son	5							30
					Robert do		Son	1							31
					David Guild		Rel.	31			S				32
					George Riddoch		Br	24			S				33
145	244 do	1		2	Wm. Jas. Smith	2	Head	37			Mar				34
					Margaret do		Wife		36		Mar	12	None		35
Total Schedules. 6	Total of Houses,	6	U — B	Total of Windowed Rooms. 11		Total Persons. 31		Total of Males. 20	Total of Females. 15	G. — G. & E. 1					

4. *Census return for Glasgow in 1911.*

Parliamentary Burgh of	Parliamentary Constituency of	Municipal Burgh ~~or Police Burgh~~ of
Glasgow	St. Rollox	Glasgow
~~Special Scavenging District of~~	~~Special Lighting District of~~	~~Island of~~

	PROFESSION OR OCCUPATION.							
	Personal Occupation.	Industry or Service with which Worker is connected.	Employer, Worker, or on Own Account.	If Working at Home.	BIRTHPLACE.	Nationality if born in a Foreign Country.	Whether 1. Totally Deaf or Deaf and Dumb. 2. Totally Blind. 3. Lunatic. 4. Imbecile or feeble-minded.	
	(q)	(r)	(s)	(t)	(u)	(v)	(w)	
1	School				Lanark Glasgow			1
2	do				do do			2
3	General Labourer 626	25 Loco Dept Rly Co	Worker		do do			3
4	Calender Worker 884	41 Calico Printers	4 do		do do			4
5	Hardware Shop 701	25	4 do		do do			5
6	Tobacco Warehouse 935	48	4 do		Ayr 03 Ayr			6
7	Electro Plater 671	26	4 do		Lanark Glasgow			7
8					do do			8
9	Clerkess 050	11 Factors	do		do do			9
10	Plumbers app. 441	28	do		do do			10
11	Message Boy 090	24 Golf Club Mfrs	do		do do			11
12	School				Argyll 0 Dunoon			12
13	do				Lanark Glasgow			13
14	do				do do			14
15					do do			15
16					do do			16
17	Cable Jointer's Asst 633	11 National Tel. Co	do		do do			17
18					do do			18
19					do do			19
20					Inverness 16 Eigg			20
21	Labourer 626	25 Loco. Builders	do		Lanark Glasgow			21
22	Joiner 210	28	4 do		Aberdeen Strathdon			22
23	Boiler Stoker 340	31 Oil & Paint Whs	do		39 South Africa C.C.	09		23
24					England 35			24
25					Lanark Glasgow			25
26	School				England 35			26
27	Brewer's Drayman 070	49 Contractor	4 do		U.S. America 40	Brit. Subj. by Parentage		27
28					Banff Banff 04			28
29	Messenger 090	40 Collar Factory	do		Renfrew Johnstone 26			29
30	School				Lanark Glasgow			30
31					do do			31
32	Railway Ticket Collector 5	13	do		Banff Banff 04			32
33	Policeman 407	22 Town Council ~~Glasgow City~~	do		Aberdeen Turriff 01			33
34	Stone Cutter 592	28	4 do		Lanark Glasgow			34
35					do do			35

Page 8]

The undermentioned Houses are situate within the Boundaries of the

Civil Parish of	*Quoad Sacra* Parish of	School Board District of	~~Parliamentary Burgh of~~	~~Parliamentary Division of~~	~~Royal Burgh~~ of
Latheron	Berriedale	Latheron			
Township ~~Municipal Burgh~~ of	~~Police Burgh of~~	~~Burgh Ward of~~	Estate ~~Town~~ of	~~Village or Hamlet of~~	~~Island of~~
			Dunbeath		

No. of Schedule	ROAD, STREET, &c., and No. or NAME of HOUSE	HOUSES: Inhabited	HOUSES: Uninhabited (U.), or Building (B.)	NAME and Surname of each Person	RELATION to Head of Family	CONDITION as to Marriage	AGE [last Birthday]: Males	AGE [last Birthday]: Females	PROFESSION or OCCUPATION	Employer	Employed	Neither Employer nor Employed, but working on own account	WHERE BORN	Gaelic, or G. & E.	Whether 1. Deaf and Dumb 2. Blind 3. Lunatic, Imbecile, or Idiot	Rooms with One or more Windows
31	Ramscraigs	1		Hugh Macleod	Head	mar	44		Farmer				Caithness-shire, Latheron	G&E		3
				Elizabeth Do.	wife	mar		44	Farmer's wife				Do. Reay			
				Donald Do.	son	—	14		Scholar				Do. Latheron			
				Margaret Do.	Daur			12	Do.				Do. Do.			
				George Do.	Son	–	9		Do.				Do. Do.			
				John G. Do.	son		6		Do.				Do. Do.			
				Elizabeth Do.	Daur			1	—				Do. Do.			
				Donald Grant	Father in Law	Widr.	~~80~~		Farmer				Do. Do.	G&E		
				George Do.	Brother in Law	Unm	47		~~Army~~ Chelsea Pensioner				Do. Do.			
				Donald Do	nephew	–	14		Scholar				Sutherlandshire, Durness			
32	Do.	1		George Gunn	Head	mar	63		Shoemaker			+	Caithness-shire, Latheron	G&E		1
				Margaret Do.	wife	mar		55	Shoemaker's wife				Do. Do.	G&E		
				George Do.	son	Unm	20		Agric. Lab.				Do. Do.	G&E		
33	Do.	1		Annie Miller	Head	Widow		57	Crofter				Do. Do.	G&E		1
				Catherine Do.	Daur	Unm		32	Housekeeper				Do. Do.	G&E		
				John Do	Son	Unm	26		Agric. Lab.		+		Do. Do.	G&E		
				Alexander Do.	son	Unm	24		Do. Do.		+		Do. Do.	G&E		
				Donald Do.	son	Unm	22		Do. Do.		+		Do. Do.	G&E		
				William Do.	grandson	–	8		Scholar				Do. Do.	G&E		
34	Do.	1		Christina McKay	Head	Unm		47	Crofter			+	Do. Do.	G&E		2
				Alexander Do.	son	Unm	20		Crofter's son		+		Do. Do.	G&E		
				Catherine Do.	Daur			14	Crofter's Daur.				Do. Do.	G&E		
				William Do.	Nephew	Unm	30		Farm Serv. (Agric Lab)		+		Do. Do.	G&E		
35	Do.	1		Marjory Munro	Head	Widow		86					Do. Do.	G&E		2
				Catherine Do.	Daur	Unm		66	Dressmaker			+	Do. Do.	G&E		
5	Total of Houses...	5	0	Total of Males and Females...			15	10					17 G&E		Total of Windowed Rooms	9

Scot.—Sheet B.]

Note.—*Draw the pen through such of the words of the headings as are inappropriate.*

5. Census return for Latheron, Caithness in 1891.

CHAPTER FOUR

Valuation Rolls, Taxation Records and Militia Lists

As well as the census returns, Scotland has many other population listings, compiled at different times to meet various needs. These records include valuation rolls, militia lists and muster rolls, and assessments for a number of taxes (hearth, poll, land, window, inhabited house, commutation, shop, male and female servants, horse, farm horse, dog, clock and watch, aid and contribution, and income taxes).

The valuation rolls and tax assessments are held by the National Records of Scotland (NRS). You'll find information on the records and their whereabouts in several booklets by Jeremy Gibson and his collaborators (see Bibliography). There's also a good deal of information about these records in the NRS book *Tracing Your Scottish Ancestors: The Official Guide*. The NRS also has free online guides to its various records at **www.nas.gov.uk/guides/default.asp**.

The 1841 census was, however, the first listing to cover the entire population. From the 1851 census onwards (and, to a certain extent, in the 1841 census), you can be reasonably sure that you've found your extended family in the census returns. This is because there are likely to be several names that tie up with those in the civil registration records.

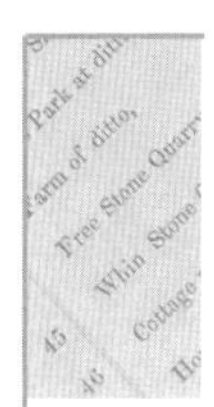

With valuation rolls, militia records and tax assessments, only the head of the household is listed with little (if any) identifying information. So, if you've found your ancestor somewhere in the 1851 census and you find someone with the same name at the same address in the 1855 valuation roll, then it's probably the same person.

If you have only the valuation roll (which is the situation in Ireland, where most of the 19th century censuses have been destroyed) or one of the other records, then you can only make an educated guess that you've found the right person.

If the records are from a period further back than you've been able to take your family tree (for example, the Poll Tax at the end of the 17th century), then you may find people with the right surname, but you won't know if they belong to your family or not (unless they have a very localised surname - and even then, you can't be absolutely sure).

Valuation rolls 1855-1989

Although there are some land valuation rolls in existence from the period before 1855, a uniform valuation of landed property throughout Scotland was not achieved until the Land Valuation (Scotland) Act of 1854. In 1989, the valuation rolls were replaced by Community Charge (which taxed individuals rather than properties) and later Council Tax, except for businesses.

Although not as useful as the census returns, valuation rolls do provide a heads-of-household listing for non-census years. Unfortunately, where annual rents were under £4, tenants may not be listed individually, but grouped together under a description such as 'small tenants' or 'sundry tenants'. In an 1855 valuation roll, you'll find:

Description (such as 'house and land')
Situation (name of place)
Proprietor (owner)
Tenant
Occupier (usually the tenant, and sometimes the proprietor)
Yearly rent or value - as estimated by assessor
Yearly rent or value - as adjusted on application or appeal
Observations

The 1896-97 valuation roll doesn't contain 'Yearly rent or value - as adjusted on application or appeal', but does have:

Inhabitant occupier not rated (another name besides the tenant)
Annual value of dwelling-house
Feu-duty or ground-annual

Valuation rolls are being added to the pay-per-view ScotlandsPeople website **www.scotlandspeople.gov.uk**, and starting with the year 1915, these will be searchable for every tenth year back to 1855, and every fifth year forward to 1955.

You can view the 1896-97 valuation roll for Dumfriesshire (minus the towns of Annan, Dumfries and Sanquhar) free of charge as part of the resources available at the Graham Maxwell Ancestry site **www.maxwellancestry.com/ancestry/resources/dumfriesshirevaluationroll.htm**.

Hearth Tax 1691-1695

The Scottish Hearth and Poll Taxes were both levied at the end of the 17th century, when Scotland still had its own parliament. The Hearth Tax was payable per hearth (the floor of the fireplace) by householders (whether landowners or tenants) from 1691-1695, which is later than in England and Wales (where a similar tax had been imposed from 1662-1689). Hospitals and the poor were exempt from the tax.

Poll Tax 1693-1699

The Poll Tax (a head tax, to be paid by both men and women) was levied in Scotland from 1693-1699 on all adults not in receipt of charity. A Poll Tax was most famously used in England and Wales in the 14th century, which led to the Peasants' Revolt in 1381, and in Britain in the 1990s (1989-1993 in Scotland) as the Community Charge, which also brought rioting in the streets.

You can find a list of Poll Tax rolls held by the National Records of Scotland in an appendix to D.J. Steel's *Sources for Scottish Genealogy and Family History* (see Bibliography).

The Aberdeen & North East Scotland Family History Society has published a series of 43 booklets containing extracts from the 'List of Pollable Persons in the Shire of Aberdeen, 1696'. You can find a list of the booklets at **http://anesfhs.org.uk/publ.htm#series3**.

Other taxes

Many other taxes were levied in the 18th century after Scotland was united with England and Wales as 'Great Britain'. These were:

- Window Tax 1747-1798 - on houses with seven windows or more;
- Commutation Tax 1784-1798 - replaced excise duties on tea;
- Inhabited House Tax 1778-1798 - annual rental of £5 or more;
- Shop Tax 1785-1789 - annual rental of £5 or more;
- Male Servants' Tax 1777-1798;
- Female Servants' Tax 1785-1792;
- Cart Tax 1785-1798;
- Carriage Tax 1785-1798;
- Horse Tax 1785-1798 - carriage and saddle horses;
- Farm Horse Tax 1797-1798 - work horses and mules;
- Dog Tax 1797-1798;
- Clock and Watch Tax 1797-1798;
- Aid and Contribution 1797-1798 - only Peeblesshire lists survive;
- Income Tax 1799-1802;
- Consolidated Schedules of Assessed Taxes 1798-1799.

You're likely to find your farming ancestors listed in the Farm Horse Tax schedules, as it was payable by most tenant farmers. You can browse the schedules online free of charge through the county or parish pages of the ScotlandsPlaces website **www.scotlandsplaces.gov.uk**.

Militia lists and muster rolls

Although the Militia Act of 1757 allowed militia regiments (reserve soldiers) to be set up in England and Wales on a county basis, the act did not apply to Scotland, coming as it did a mere 11 years after the Jacobite Rebellion of 'Bonnie Prince Charlie' in 1745-46. However, by 1797, over 50 years had passed since 'the 45' and the threat of an attack by French forces under Napoleon Bonaparte allowed the British Government to countenance raising militia regiments in Scotland too.

As well as militia regiments, which served mainly in Scotland, there were also 'fencibles' (in defence of the realm) who also served in England and Ireland (although militia regiments could do this too). Militia regiments were raised by ballot, while fencibles were volunteers (as were locally raised volunteer corps).

The British Government allowed the Duke of Argyll and the Earl of Sutherland (whose loyalty to the Hanoverian Crown was not in doubt) to raise fencible regiments in 1759 and 1778 (which were disbanded in 1763 and 1783 respectively). The Gordon Fencibles were also first raised in 1778 and disbanded in 1783.

Many more fencibles came into being towards the end of the 18th century: 17 regiments were raised in 1793 or 1794, and a further seven in 1798 or 1799. Many of those raised in the early 1790s were disbanded in 1799, most of the rest in 1802 and the last remaining fencible regiment - the Prince of Wales's (Aberdeen Highland) Regiment - in 1803.

Most of the Scottish militia records are held by the NRS, while you'll find the remainder either in the National Library of Scotland (NLS), various Scottish local archives or at The National Archives (TNA) at Kew in London.

You can read more about militias, fencibles and volunteers (and the location of their records) in Professor Arnold Morrison's self-published booklet *Some Scottish Sources on Militias, Fencibles and Volunteer Corps,* which you can read online free of charge at **www.scribd.com/doc/68100606/The-Defence-of-Scotland-Militias-Fencibles-and-Volunteer-Corps1793-1820**. In addition, *Militia Lists and Musters 1757-1876*, a booklet by Jeremy Gibson and Mervyn Medlycott, includes several pages on the location of lists of Scottish militia, fencibles and volunteers.

At the Findmypast subscription/pay-per-view website **www.findmypast.co.uk**, you can view militia records for the period 1806-1915 that are held by TNA in its WO96 collection. Fencible records are in the WO97 collection.

The Scottish Archive Network (SCAN) has made the Lieutenancy Book of Roxburghshire (with lists of men balloted to serve in the militia) available free of charge at **www.scan.org.uk/researchrtools/lieutenancy.htm**.

You can view the 1802 militia survey for Perth at the subscription site Ancestry.co.uk **www.ancestry.co.uk**, which aims to list all men between 18 and 45 years of age. In addition, the free Friends of Perth & Kinross Archives pages **www.pkc.gov.uk/Education+and+learning/Libraries+archives+and+learning+centres/Archives/Friends+of+the+archives** have a Perthshire militia collection that includes petitions from c1704-1859 (but mainly from 1790-1810), certifications from 1802-1810 and assorted militia papers from 1680-1891 (but mainly from 1785-1820).

In the library of the Society of Genealogists

You'll find several Scottish Hearth Tax, Poll Tax and other published lists at the Society's library (see Chapter 16).

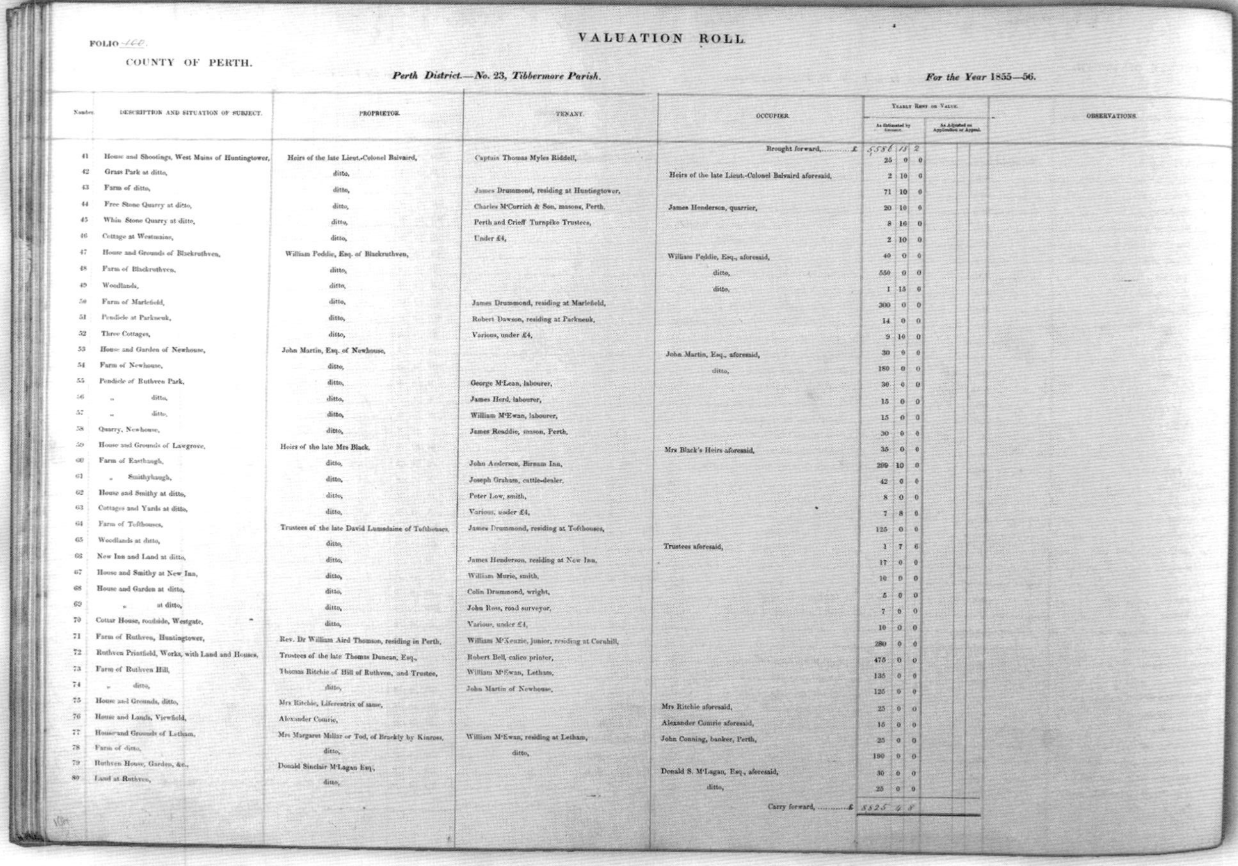

FOLIO 160.

VALUATION ROLL

COUNTY OF PERTH.

Perth District.—No. 23, Tibbermore Parish.

For the Year 1855—56.

Number.	DESCRIPTION AND SITUATION OF SUBJECT.	PROPRIETOR.	TENANT.	OCCUPIER.	YEARLY RENT OR VALUE. As Estimated by Assessor. £	s	d	As Adjusted on Application or Appeal.	OBSERVATIONS.
				Brought forward,............£	5586	15	2		
41	House and Shootings, West Mains of Huntingtower,	Heirs of the late Lieut.-Colonel Balvaird,	Captain Thomas Myles Riddell,		25	0	0		
42	Grass Park at ditto,	ditto,		Heirs of the late Lieut.-Colonel Balvaird aforesaid,	2	10	0		
43	Farm of ditto,	ditto,	James Drummond, residing at Huntingtower,		71	10	0		
44	Free Stone Quarry at ditto,	ditto,	Charles M'Currich & Son, masons, Perth,	James Henderson, quarrier,	20	10	0		
45	Whin Stone Quarry at ditto,	ditto,	Perth and Crieff Turnpike Trustees,		8	16	0		
46	Cottage at Westmains,	ditto,	Under £4,		2	10	0		
47	House and Grounds of Blackruthven,	William Peddie, Esq. of Blackruthven,		William Peddie, Esq., aforesaid,	40	0	0		
48	Farm of Blackruthven,	ditto,		ditto,	550	0	0		
49	Woodlands,	ditto,		ditto,	1	15	0		
50	Farm of Marlefield,	ditto,	James Drummond, residing at Marlefield,		300	0	0		
51	Pendicle at Parkneuk,	ditto,	Robert Dawson, residing at Parkneuk,		14	0	0		
52	Three Cottages,	ditto,	Various, under £4,		9	10	0		
53	House and Garden of Newhouse,	John Martin, Esq. of Newhouse,		John Martin, Esq., aforesaid,	30	0	0		
54	Farm of Newhouse,	ditto,		ditto,	180	0	0		
55	Pendicle of Ruthven Park,	ditto,	George M'Lean, labourer,		30	0	0		
56	" ditto,	ditto,	James Herd, labourer,		15	0	0		
57	" ditto,	ditto,	William M'Ewan, labourer,		15	0	0		
58	Quarry, Newhouse,	ditto,	James Readdie, mason, Perth,		30	0	0		
59	House and Grounds of Lawgrove,	Heirs of the late Mrs Black,		Mrs Black's Heirs aforesaid,	35	0	0		
60	Farm of Easthaugh,	ditto,	John Anderson, Birnam Inn,		299	10	0		
61	" Smithyhaugh,	ditto,	Joseph Graham, cattle-dealer,		42	0	0		
62	House and Smithy at ditto,	ditto,	Peter Low, smith,		8	0	0		
63	Cottages and Yards at ditto,	ditto,	Various, under £4,		7	8	0		
64	Farm of Tofthouses,	Trustees of the late David Lumsdaine of Tofthouses,	James Drummond, residing at Tofthouses,		125	0	0		
65	Woodlands at ditto,	ditto,		Trustees aforesaid,	1	7	6		
66	New Inn and Land at ditto,	ditto,	James Henderson, residing at New Inn,		17	0	0		
67	House and Smithy at New Inn,	ditto,	William Murie, smith,		10	0	0		
68	House and Garden at ditto,	ditto,	Colin Drummond, wright,		5	0	0		
69	" at ditto,	ditto,	John Ross, road surveyor,		7	0	0		
70	Cottar House, roadside, Westgate,	ditto,	Various, under £4,		10	0	0		
71	Farm of Ruthven, Huntingtower,	Rev. Dr William Aird Thomson, residing in Perth,	William M'Kenzie, junior, residing at Cornhill,		280	0	0		
72	Ruthven Printfield, Works, with Land and Houses,	Trustees of the late Thomas Duncan, Esq.,	Robert Bell, calico printer,		475	0	0		
73	Farm of Ruthven Hill,	Thomas Ritchie of Hill of Ruthven, and Trustee,	William M'Ewan, Letham,		135	0	0		
74	" ditto,	ditto,	John Martin of Newhouse,		125	0	0		
75	House and Grounds, ditto,	Mrs Ritchie, Liferentrix of same,		Mrs Ritchie aforesaid,	25	0	0		
76	House and Lands, Viewfield,	Alexander Comrie,		Alexander Comrie aforesaid,	15	0	0		
77	House and Grounds of Letham,	Mrs Margaret Millar or Tod, of Brackly by Kinross,	William M'Ewan, residing at Letham,	John Conning, banker, Perth,	25	0	0		
78	Farm of ditto,	ditto,	ditto,		190	0	0		
79	Ruthven House, Garden, &c.,	Donald Sinclair M'Lagan Esq.,		Donald S. M'Lagan, Esq., aforesaid,	30	0	0		
80	Land at Ruthven,	ditto,		ditto,	25	0	0		
				Carry forward,............£	5525	4	8		

6. Valuation roll for Tibbermore, Perthshire in 1855.

CHAPTER FIVE
Parish Registers

Before civil registration of births, marriages and deaths began in Scotland in 1855, baptisms, marriages and burials were recorded in the parish registers of the Church of Scotland. Today the Church of Scotland is a Presbyterian Protestant church (and the main church in Scotland), but when the order was given in 1552 to record these life events, it was part of the Roman Catholic Church.

The Church of Scotland changed from Roman Catholicism to a Presbyterian form of Protestantism in 1560. The church is organised on the basis of a number of courts: at parish level, you have the kirk session (composed of the minister and 'elders' of the church), and at district level, the presbytery. At national level, there's the General Assembly, which is chaired by a Moderator who is elected for just one year. There are no bishops or archbishops in Presbyterian churches.

Kirk session records are held by the National Records of Scotland (NRS) in Edinburgh. There are some kirk session entries in the parish registers, and a few baptisms, marriages and burials recorded in the kirk session registers. The kirk session records (about five million pages of information) have been digitised and are available to view at the NRS and at many archives around Scotland. The records are expected to be made available online at some point in the future, probably via the ScotlandsPeople website.

The only parish in Scotland that actually began to record baptisms in 1553 was Errol in southern Perthshire, and there are only two for that year: the baptisms of Christian Hay on 27 December and David Barrie on 29 December. The first Scottish marriages were not recorded until 1555, also in the parish of Errol.

Although the first burial in Scotland was not recorded until 1560 in Aberdeen City (that of Andrew Culley), earlier burials were later recorded for Aberdeen City (Isabell Culley nee Anderson had been buried in 1538, and William Coupar in 1539).

For the parish of Anstruther Wester, also in Fife, there is a 'register of deaths of persons belonging to this parish … collected in the 19th century by the Revd. Hew Scott from the testament registers of the commissariots of Edinburgh and St. Andrews, the tombstones in the churchyard and other sources', beginning with three deaths in 1549 (William Waucht; Catharine Smart, wife of Thomas Elis; and Katharine Steinsoun, spouse of Thomas Wricht).

It wasn't until much later that many parishes started to keep records of baptisms, marriages (or proclamations of banns), and burials, especially in the Highlands and islands. On the Isle of Skye, for instance, the earliest register was for the parish of Portree, beginning in 1800. As if that's not bad enough, about a third of Scottish parishes didn't record burials at all.

There are no bishops' transcripts of the Scottish parish registers. Whereas in England and Wales, register copies were sent to the bishop of the relevant diocese, the Church of Scotland had no bishops most of the time after it became Presbyterian in 1560.

As well as the nonconformist churches (such as Baptists and Methodists) that you find in England and Wales from the 17th century onwards, Scotland has its own secession churches - Presbyterian churches that broke away from the Church of Scotland particularly during the 18th and 19th centuries. Nonconformist and secession churches are covered in the next chapter.

Unfortunately, with large numbers of people worshipping at other churches, and also because of a charge that was imposed briefly at the end of the 18th century, very many baptisms, marriages and burials were not recorded in the Church of Scotland registers. Not only did this apply in the large cities such as Glasgow and Edinburgh, but also in remote areas like the county of Sutherland.

For the Glasgow entry in the *New Statistical Account of Scotland*, Dr. James Cleland (co-author of the city's entry in 1845) wrote to ask each of its 75 clergymen asking how many baptisms they had performed in 1830. In the Glasgow account, Dr.

Cleland wrote, 'It appeared that in the city and suburbs, there were 6,397 children baptized, and of that number there were only 3,225 inserted in the parochial registers, leaving unregistered 3,172.'

Dr. Cleland was shocked that the state of the parish registers in Edinburgh was very much the same as in Glasgow.

'While the great importance of accurate Parochial registers is admitted by all, it is astonishing how little they have been attended to in this country,' he said. 'In Edinburgh, the metropolis of Scotland, a city distinguished for its erudition, and for its numerous and valuable institutions, the baptismal register is miserably defective.

'It appears from a printed report of a Committee of the Town Council of that city, of date 20th February, that in 1834, the baptismal register for the thirteen parishes contained only the names of 480 children.'

This state of affairs is illustrated in the ScotlandsPeople online database, which holds records of far fewer baptisms that took place in Scotland during 1854, compared to births registered in 1855. A comparison of baptism and births in Scotland's 33 historic counties is shown in the following table:

County	Baptisms in 1854	Births in 1855
Aberdeenshire	5,054	6,679
Angus (Forfarshire)	3,099	6,384
Argyll	1,455	2,047
Ayrshire	3,141	6,951
Banffshire	1,189	1,621
Berwickshire	815	1,102
Bute	229	403
Caithness	648	1,138
Clackmannanshire	361	615
Dumfriesshire	1,455	2,431
Dunbartonshire	784	1,698
East Lothian (Haddingtonshire)	785	1,170
Fife	3,255	4,978
Inverness-shire	832	2,383
Kincardineshire	813	1,068
Kinross-shire	124	242
Kirkcudbrightshire	696	1,177
Lanarkshire	7339	23,009
Midlothian (Edinburghshire)	5,154	7,827

Moray (Elginshire)	996	1,554
Nairnshire	168	213
Orkney	817	807
Peeblesshire	208	329
Perthshire	2,551	3,293
Renfrewshire	1,668	5,615
Ross & Cromarty	591	2,143
Roxburghshire	793	1,650
Selkirkshire	180	330
Shetland	893	824
Stirlingshire	1,534	2,986
Sutherland	131	615
West Lothian (Linlithgowshire)	512	1,323
Wigtownshire	745	1,140
TOTAL	48,868	95,367

You can see in the table that the number of births recorded in Scotland in 1855 was almost twice the number of Church of Scotland baptisms just one year earlier. This was the situation in most counties, although in Orkney and Shetland the number of baptisms in 1854 had been greater than the number of births the following year.

The counties with the worst record for recording baptisms were the Highland counties of Inverness-shire, Ross & Cromarty and Sutherland (probably because the unrecorded baptisms took place in the Free Church) and the western counties of Dunbartonshire, Lanarkshire, and Renfrewshire (with the 'missing' baptisms probably spread between the secession churches and the Roman Catholic Church, because of the many people living in that area who had migrated from Ireland).

In 1855, the new General Register Office for Scotland (GROS) called in the Church of Scotland parish registers up to the end of 1854, which are known as the Old Parochial or Old Parish Registers (OPRs). The registers are held in New Register House in Edinburgh, with indexed images of all existing records of baptisms, marriages/banns and burials accessible at the pay-per-view ScotlandsPeople website **www.scotlandspeople.gov.uk**

Indexes of the baptisms and marriages are also searchable free of charge on the LDS Church's Family Search site **https://www.familysearch.org**. Although the LDS database of Scottish births/baptisms supposedly begins in 1564, I searched it for the period 1538-1563 and received 950 results, including the two Errol baptisms in 1553 (and a few records apparently going back to 1506). In addition, while the cut-off year for the database is supposed to be 1950, there are a few later records.

Likewise, the LDS database of Scottish marriages is supposed to cover the years 1561-1910, but there are actually 214 earlier records, starting in 1555 (and also one apparently from 1528 in the Burgher Church in Dalry, Ayrshire, although there was no Burgher Church until the 18th century). There are also 86 records in the database for marriages that took place after 1910, right up to 1956.

Scottish parish registers (as well as those of England and Wales) are being transcribed, indexed and made available online free of charge by the FreeREG Project **www.freereg.org.uk**.

Scottish parish register entries don't contain as much information as you'll find in the civil registration records. In a baptismal record, you're likely to find:

- name of the child;
- names of both parents, including the mother's maiden name (although sometimes no mother's name is given at all);
- date of baptism (and sometimes the date of birth too);
- father's occupation (in urban areas);
- address of the parents (but this can be quite general);
- if the child was illegitimate (this tends to be in earlier records).

You'll sometimes find the name of the father of the bride in a marriage entry, but not the name of the groom's father. Many of the entries in the registers are not of the marriages themselves, but are records of the proclamation of banns before the marriage (announcing the intention to marry). Often there's no proof that the marriage did actually take place, although if banns were proclaimed and then several children are born, it's very unlikely that there was no marriage.

A woman's burial record may mention her husband, and a child's the father, but a man's burial record will usually tell you very little. The register of the parish of Stow, Midlothian, however, does state that:

> 'James Neil in Crookston Mill perished on the road from Dalkeith at the 15th milestone on the night of the 13th February 1826 and was buried on the 18th following [and] had the second [-best] mortcloth [covering the coffin], aged 22.'

The standardised pre-printed form registers introduced in England and Wales for recording marriages from 1754 onwards, and baptisms and burials from 1813 onwards, didn't apply to Scotland and weren't used there. You will therefore find considerable variation between parishes in the appearance of the register entries, as well as their content.

Scottish names

In Scotland, a naming pattern used to be followed, which saw the first son named after his paternal grandfather, the second after his maternal grandfather, and the third after his father. Similarly, the first daughter was named after her maternal grandmother, the second after her paternal grandmother, and the third after her mother. The Scottish Naming Pattern can be helpful in researching your family, but you have to bear in mind that it wasn't always strictly followed, particularly where there was illegitimacy.

Some forenames were considered interchangeable, so that you may find 'Jean' as 'Janet', or 'Daniel' as 'Donald', or 'Peter' as 'Patrick'. Also, there are Gaelic versions of English-language forenames, such as 'Alistair' for 'Alexander', 'Hamish' for 'James' and 'Ian' for 'John'. Even my own surname of 'Stewart' can be written as 'Stiùbhard' in Gaelic!

In the Highland and islands, patronymics survived into the 18th century (the 19th in Shetland). Under the patronymic system, instead of a fixed surname, a man or woman would use the forename of his or her father as a second name with 'son of' or 'daughter of'. The patronymic changed with each generation (and this is what still happens today in Iceland). As my father's forename was William, I would be Alan MacWilliam, rather than Alan Stewart.

In Scotland, the use of a different patronymic in each generation died out, being replaced by a patronymic-style surname (such as MacDonald or MacKenzie), which doesn't change with each generation.

The 20 most common surnames in Scotland around 1855-1858 were:

1. Smith
2. MacDonald/McDonald
3. Brown
4. Robertson
5. Thomson
6. Stewart
7. Campbell
8. Wilson
9. Anderson
10. MacKay/McKay
11. MacKenzie/McKenzie
12. Scott

13. Johnston
14. Miller
15. Reid
16. Ross
17. Paterson
18. Fraser
19. Murray
20. MacLean/McLean

You can find surveys of Scotland's most common surnames over the years at the GROS website **www.gro-scotland.gov.uk/statistics/theme/vital-events/births/popular-names/surnames-in-scotland-over-the-last-140-years.html**.

Scottish counties and parishes

Some of the historic Scottish counties (those in existence before the local government re-organisation of 1975) had previously had other names. In 1890, Edinburghshire and Dumbartonshire officially became Midlothian and Dunbartonshire respectively, and the separate counties of Ross-shire and Cromartyshire became one county as Ross & Cromarty.

In 1918, Elginshire became Moray; in 1921, Haddingtonshire became East Lothian; in 1924, Linlithgowshire became West Lothian; and in 1928, Forfarshire became Angus. The island county of Shetland was also known as Zetland until 1975.

The boundaries of Scottish counties were altered in 1891, so that there were no detached parts of counties (other than the eastern part of Dunbartonshire between Stirlingshire and Lanarkshire). This meant that, for example, the detached part of Perthshire containing the parishes of Culross and Tulliallan became part of Fife, and the detached parish of Alva was removed from Stirlingshire and added to Clackmannanshire.

At the same time, parishes that had been in more than one county had their boundaries changed (or the county boundaries were changed) so that they were located in only one county. The parish of Arngask, for instance, which had previously been split between Fife, Kinross-shire and Perthshire, was situated entirely in Perthshire from 1891 onwards.

In the library of the Society of Genealogists

You'll find many Scottish parish registers on microfilm at the Society's library. All are listed (according to the old pre-1975 counties) on the free online catalogue available through the Society's website.

A. D. 1784.

Oct. 3. John Dun Smith Ancrum had a Son Baptis-
ed Adam. and a Daughter Baptised Betty.
Nov. 21st Geo. Richardson younger in Longn a Dr. Bap. Allison.
1785. Jany 26. Stephen Balmer, Brother to Walter Balmer
Tennant Longn had a Dr. B. Janet. Born 14th Curt.
Feb. 8. Wm Hislop Carrier in Ancrum a Son B. Thomas
Mar. 11th Patrick Smith Taylor in Do a Dr. B. Anne. Born the
8th Ultimo.
Mar. 20. William Rutherford Tent in Ancrum mains had a
Daughter Bapd Janet.
Apr. 3d John Wight householder in Ancrum a Dr. B. Isabel.
Do. 15. John Smith Son in Law to Thomas Currie Portion-
er of Ancrum, had a Son Bapd John
May 22. Mungo Pasoun Tent Wellig a Son Bap. William.
July 17th John Riddel Servant at Caverton mains and
householder in Ancrum, had a Son Bapd Robert.
Augt 7. William Younger Shoemaker in Longnewtoun
had a Son Baptised John
Sep. 25. Stephen Balmer Servant and Householder at Easter
Barnhills, had a Son Bapd William.
Oct. 9 Geo. Finlis Gardner in Ancrum had a Daughter Bap-
tised Isabel, Born the 26 Augt Last
Do. 30. James Kennedy Labourer in Ancrum had a Son
Baptised Nancy.
Nov. 5. Arthur Hope Labourer in Ancrum had a
Son Bap. James. Born 31 Augt Last.
Do. 27. Gideon Robson, Weaver Barnhills, had a Son Bap-
tised George
[illegible] James Inglis labourer in Ancrum had a
Son Baptised John

7. Old Parish Register baptisms for Ancrum, Roxburghshire in 1733.

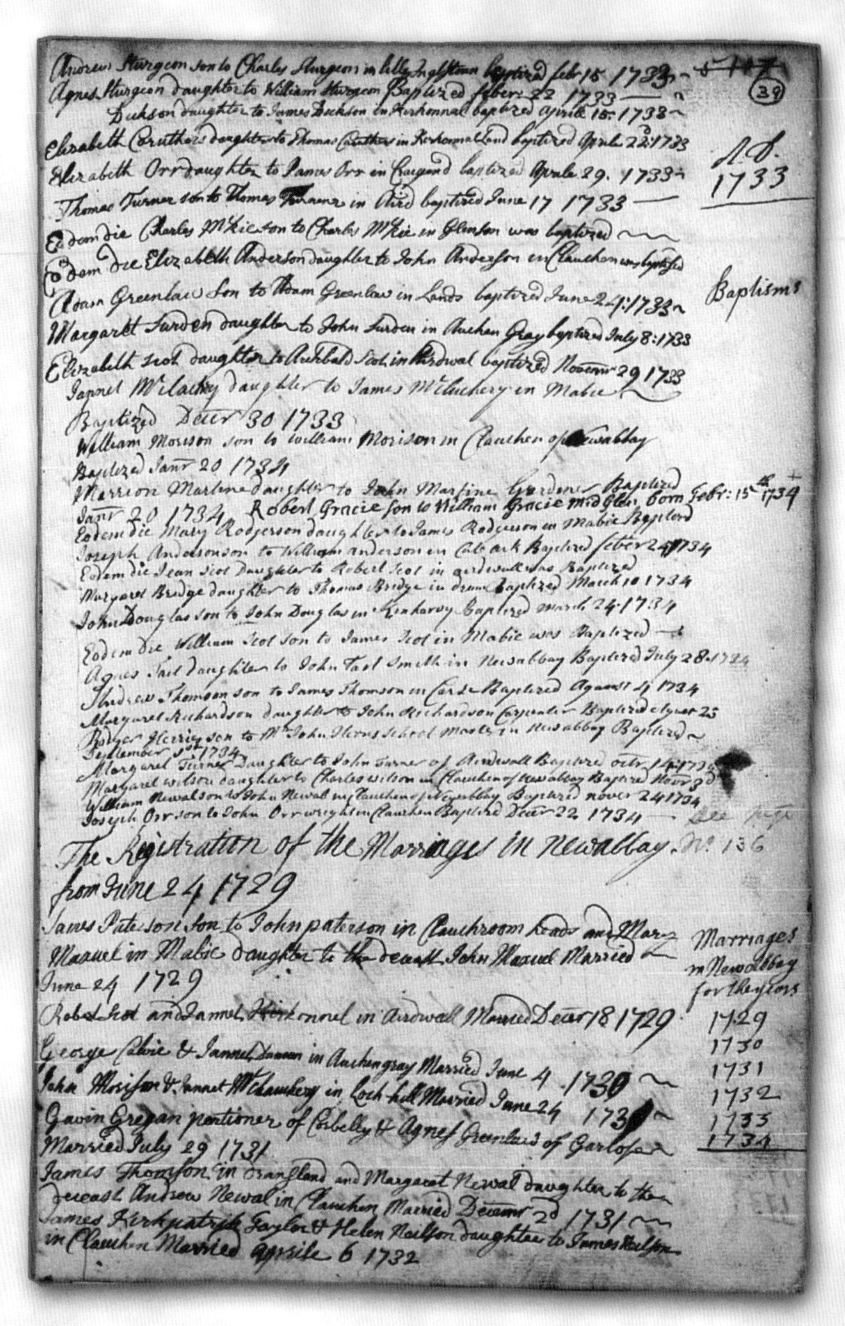
Andrew Sturgeon son to Charles Sturgeon in [illegible] baptized febr 15 1733
Agnes Sturgeon daughter to William Sturgeon Baptized feber 22 1733
Dickson daughter to James Dickson in Kirkonnal baptized aprile 15 1733
Elizabeth Caruthers daughter to Thomas Caruthers in Kirkonnal [illegible] baptized Aprile 22 1733
Elizabeth Orr daughter to James Orr in [illegible] baptized Aprile 29. 1733
Thomas Turner son to Thomas Turner in [illegible] baptized June 17 1733
Eodem die Charles McKie son to Charles McKie in [illegible] was baptized
Eodem die Elizabeth Anderson daughter to John Anderson in Clauchen was baptized
Adam Greenlaw son to Adam Greenlaw in Lands baptized June 24 1733
Margaret Surden daughter to John Surden in Auchen Gray baptized July 8 1733
Elizabeth Scot daughter to Archibald Scot in Ardwal baptized Novemr 29 1733
Jannet McLachy daughter to James McLachery in Mabie Baptized Decr 30 1733
William Morison son to William Morison in Clauchen of Newabbay Baptized Janr 20 1734
Marrion Martine daughter to John Martine Gardener Baptized Janr 20 1734 Robert Gracie son to William Gracie Mid Glen born Febr 15th 1734
Eodem die Mary Rodgerson daughter to James Rodgerson in Mabie Baptized
Joseph Anderson son to William Anderson in [illegible] Baptized feber 24 1734
Eodem die Jean Scot daughter to Robert Scot in Ardwall was Baptized
Margaret Bridge daughter to Thomas Bridge in drum Baptized March 10 1734
John Douglas son to John Douglas in Kinharvy Baptized march 24 1734
Eodem die William Scot son to James Scot in Mabie was Baptized
Agnes Tait daughter to John Tait Smith in Newabbay Baptized July 28 1734
Andrew Thomson son to James Thomson in [illegible] Baptized August 4 1734
Margaret Richardson daughter to John Richardson Carpenter Baptized August 25
Rodger Herries son to Mr John Herries School Master in Newabbay Baptized September 1st 1734
Margaret Turner daughter to John Turner of Ardwall Baptized octr 14 1734
Margaret Wilson daughter to Charles Wilson in Clauchen of Newabbay Baptized Novr 3
William Newal son to John Newal in Clauchen of Newabbay Baptized Novr 24 1734
Joseph Orr son to John Orr wright in Clauchen Baptized Decr 22 1734

The Registration of the Marriages in Newabbay from June 24 1729

James Paterson son to John Paterson in Clauchroom head and Mary Maxwel in Mabie daughter to the deceast John Maxwel Married June 24 1729
Robert Scot and Jannet Kirkonnel in Ardwall Married Decr 18 1729
George Cabrie & Jannet [illegible] in Auchengray Married June 4 1730
John Morison & Jannet McChamberry in Loch hill Married June 24 1730
Gavin Gregan portioner of [illegible] & Agnes Greenlees of Garloff Married July 29 1731
James Thomson in [illegible] and Margaret Newal daughter to the deceast Andrew Newal in Clauchen Married Decemr 2d 1731
James Kirkpatrick Taylor & Helen Neilson daughter to James Neilson in Clauchen Married Aprile 6 1732

(39)
A.D. 1733
Baptisms
See page No. 136
Marriages in Newabbay for the years 1729 1730 1731 1732 1733 1734

8. Old Parish Register baptisms and marriages for New Abbey, Kirkcudbrightshire in 1731.

CHAPTER SIX
Other Church Registers

As well as the Church of Scotland, there are many other Scottish churches, including the:

1. Roman Catholic Church;
2. Scottish Episcopal Church (part of the Anglican family of churches);
3. Nonconformist churches that spread north from England and Wales (such as the Baptist, Congregational and Methodist churches, as well as 'Quaker' meetings);
5. Presbyterian 'secession' churches that broke away from the Church of Scotland over doctrinal differences.

As mentioned in the previous chapter, after the Church of Scotland broke with the Roman Catholic Church in 1560, it formally adopted a Presbyterian structure in 1592. This involved the abolition of bishops and archbishops, but King James I (VI of Scotland) re-introduced them during the 17th century, and his son King Charles I brought in the use of an Anglican-style prayer book.

Many people in Scotland were unhappy with this, and in 1638, a 'National Covenant' was signed at Greyfriars Church in Edinburgh in 1638. These 'covenanters' were persecuted until the Glorious Revolution in 1688, when the Roman Catholic King James II (VII of Scotland) was replaced by the

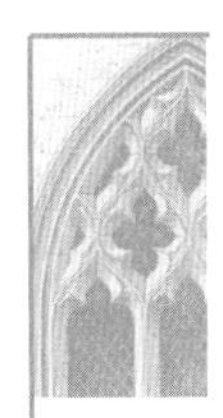

Protestant King William III (II of Scotland) and Queen Mary II (II of both countries).

In 1690, the Church of Scotland became Presbyterian once more, and the Scottish Episcopal Church was formed by those who wished to continue to worship in an Anglican church. At the same time, some of the former covenanters didn't want to be part of the Church of Scotland and set up the Reformed Presbyterian Church of Scotland (also known as the 'Cameronians').

Microfilmed and digitised copies of many of the registers of the above churches are held by the National Records of Scotland (NRS). To find out which records are at the NRS and which are elsewhere, you can search the catalogues of the NRS **www.nas.gov.uk/onlineCatalogue**, the Scottish Archive Network (SCAN) **www.scan.org.uk/catalogue** (with information from over 50 Scottish local archives) and the National Register of Archives for Scotland (NRAS) **www.nas.gov.uk/onlineRegister** (which contains information on records in private hands). More detail follows in each section below.

Roman Catholic Church

With 24% of the Christian population of Scotland according to the 2001 census, the Roman Catholic Church is strong once again, despite over 400 years of Protestantism (the last 300 of which were dominated by Presbyterianism). This Roman Catholic strength is due in large part to migration from Ireland in the 19th century.

At the Scottish Catholic Archives (SCA) website **www.scottishcatholicarchives.org.uk**, you'll find a list of the Scottish Roman Catholic parishes for which it holds registers. These can be viewed free of charge at the SCA in Columba House, Edinburgh. Images of all the records (baptisms, marriages, burials and other records) are available online at the pay-per-view ScotlandsPeople website **www.scotlandspeople.gov.uk**.

Baptisms cover the period 1703-1992, marriages 1736-1934 and burials 1742-1955. The other records 1742-1909 are lists of communicants, confessions, confirmations, seat rents, sick visits and *status animarum* ('state of the souls') lists of all Roman Catholics in a given area.

As well as the parish registers, the online records include the registers of Glasgow Dalbeth and Edinburgh Mount Vernon cemeteries, and also the baptism, marriage, burial and other records of the Catholic Bishopric of the Forces, covering British armed forces throughout the world.

Searching the online catalogue of the NRS for 'RH21' will tell you which Roman Catholic records it holds. To find out which other repositories hold Catholic records, you should search the catalogues of SCAN and the NRAS.

Scottish Episcopal Church

During the late 16th century and almost all of the 17th, Episcopalians (i.e. those who supported a church with bishops and archbishops) represented a faction within the Church of Scotland in opposition to the Presbyterians, rather than a separate denomination. During the 17th century, the Church of Scotland was alternately Presbyterian and Episcopalian.

It was only after the Revolution Settlement of 1690 that the Scottish Episcopal Church was founded as a separate Scottish church. In much of the 18th century, however, Scottish Episcopalians were persecuted because of their support for the Jacobite pretenders, rather than the Hanoverian monarch.

Searching the online catalogue of the NRS for 'CH12' will let you know which Scottish Episcopal Church records it holds. To find out which other repositories hold Episcopal records, you should search the catalogues of SCAN and the NRAS.

You can also find listings by county of the pre-1855 Scottish Episcopal Church registers (and their post-1855 continuation) held by the National Records of Scotland (NRS) in D.J. Steel's *Sources for Scottish Genealogy and Family History* (see Bibliography).

Nonconformist churches from England and Wales

The first Baptist congregation was established in 1652 in Leith, consisting partly of English soldiers, but virtually disappeared after the withdrawal of the English Army from Scotland in 1659. There was a Baptist revival a century later and by 1835 most counties had Baptist churches and the Scotch Baptist Association (later the Baptist Union of Scotland) was founded.

The earliest Society of Friends ('Quaker') meeting was founded in 1653 in Lanarkshire, but persecution followed and the Scots Quaker Act of 1661 prohibited meetings. Records of the Aberdeen Monthly Meeting began in 1672, however, and the 1661 Act was rescinded as part of the Revolution Settlement. After that, Quakers were generally tolerated (although there were attacks by mobs in Edinburgh and Glasgow), but never very successful in Scotland. The Library at Friends House in London has some information on Scottish Quakers.

Methodist Societies were founded in 1755 in Dunbar in East Lothian, and in 1764 in Edinburgh. The following year, circuits were established in Aberdeen, Glasgow, Edinburgh and Dundee, with Dunbar following in 1766, Inverness in 1779 and Ayr in 1786. Methodism was not a success in Scotland, however, with 1819 being its peak year in the 19th century (with nearly 3,800 members), as there were few preachers and an expensive chapel-building programme had been launched. In the 20th century, numbers did rise, in part through English migration.

Congregationalism began in Scotland at the end of the 18th century and beginning of the 19th, when 85 churches were founded. In 1812, 55 of those churches joined together as the Congregational Union of Scotland, which merged in 1897 with the Evangelical Union, another nonconformist church, which had been founded in 1843.

Like Methodism, Unitarianism was not particularly popular in Scotland. Although there had been some mission work in the late 18th century, there are only four congregations in the large cities today (and one 'fellowship' in Orkney). The oldest of the present congregations was established in Edinburgh in 1776, and the Scottish Unitarian Association was founded in 1813.

Searching the online catalogue of the NRS for 'CH10' will let you know which 'Quaker' records it holds. Alternatively, you should search for 'CH11' for Methodist, 'CH14' for Congregational and 'CH15' for Unitarian records. To find out which other repositories hold records of these churches (and Baptist churches), you should search the catalogues of SCAN and the NRAS.

Presbyterian secession churches

From the end of the 17th century, many churches broke away from the Church of Scotland, and these secession churches suffered a series of further splits during the 18th, 19th and even 20th centuries. You'll find a diagram illustrating this and the subsequent re-unions at **http://haygenealogy.com/hay/church/churchchart.jpg**.

In 1733, the Original Secession Church (or Associate Presbytery) was founded by the Revd. Ebenezer Erskine and others, as they didn't agree that landowners should be able to appoint ministers to the churches on their estates (a system known as 'patronage').

In 1747, the Original Secession Church divided into 'Burghers' (the Associate Synod) and 'Anti-Burghers' (the General Associate Synod) over the requirement of city dignitaries known as burgesses to take an oath acknowledging the 'true religion'.

The Burghers and Anti-Burghers both divided into 'Auld Lichts' (Old Lights) and 'New Lichts' (New Lights) in 1799 and 1806 respectively. It was the belief of the Auld Lichts that the state should support the church (this was known as 'establishmentarianism'), while the New Lichts believed that the church and the state should be quite independent of each another (known as 'disestablishmentarianism' or 'voluntaryism').

Before the divisions into Auld and New Lichts, however, the Church of Scotland had expelled the Revd. Thomas Gillespie also over patronage. In 1761, Gillespie and two colleagues formed the Presbytery of Relief (the Relief Church).

Eighty years later, patronage was still an issue, especially in the Highlands. In 1843, there occurred the largest of the secessions, which was so big it was called the 'Disruption'. This was caused by the Revd. Thomas Chalmers and over 450 other ministers (this was a third of the total number), who left the Church of Scotland to form a new Free Church of Scotland, which had 900 congregations by 1851.

Reunification of the secession churches

After the secessions mentioned above, many of the breakaway churches united with other seceders. In most cases, there remained a 'continuing church' when some of the congregations of one or other of the amalgamating churches chose not to merge with the other.

Even before the Disruption of 1843, 154 of the New Licht Burgher congregations merged in 1820 with 129 of the New Licht Anti-Burghers as the United Secession Church. Almost 20 years after that, the Auld Licht Burghers decided to rejoin the Church of Scotland, while the Auld Licht Anti-Burghers continued to exist as the Original Secession Church.

There was a further union in 1847, when all the United Secession Church congregations and 118 of the 136 Relief Church congregations merged as the United Presbyterian Church, which had 465 congregations by 1851.

In the following year, the Original Secession Church joined the Free Church, and in 1876, the Reformed Presbyterian Church (the Cameronians) did the same (but in both cases, minorities remained outside the unions). Some members of the Free Church broke away in 1893 to form the Free Presbyterian Church.

In 1900, after many years of negotiation, the United Presbyterian Church and the Free Church merged as the United Free Church (although 25 Free Church ministers and 63 congregations mainly in Gaelic-speaking areas - and known in Scotland as the 'wee Frees' - did not join the merged church), which rejoined the Church of Scotland in 1929 (although, once again, a minority in the United Free Church remained outside).

More recently, the Associated Presbyterian Churches seceded from the Free Presbyterian Church in 1989, and the Free Church Continuing broke away from the Free Church in 2000. With all its secessions and reunions, it's hardly surprising that Scotland has been described as the most 'reformed' nation of the Reformation!

According to the *Ordnance Gazetteer of Scotland* (Thomas C. Jack, 1885), the size of the principal churches in the late 19th century was:

Church group	No. of archbishops and (bishops)	No. of parishes/ congregations and (clergy)	No. of members or communicants*
Church of Scotland	-	1,293	515,786*
Free Church of Scotland	-	(1,104)	300,000+
United Presbyterian Church	-	558 (594)	178,195
Roman Catholic Church	2 (4)	305 (324)	c.321,000
Scottish Episcopal Church	(7)	294 (267)	84,664
Baptists	-	89 (80)	8,643
Congregationalists	-	86	
Evangelical Union	-	86	
Wesleyan Methodists	-	(43) + 99 lay preachers	6,000 1,000* + 500 Primitive Methodists

Church records held by the NRS

You can find the records of many of the secession churches by searching the NRS online catalogue for 'CH3'. Alternatively, searching for 'CH16' or 'CH13' will let you know respectively which records of the Free Church or United Free Church of Scotland it holds. To find out which other repositories hold records of these churches, you should search the catalogues of SCAN and the NRAS.

D. J. Steel's *Sources for Scottish Genealogy and Family History* contains listings by county of the NRS's pre-1855 registers (and their post-1855 continuation) of the seceding Presbyterian churches (as well as those of the Scottish Episcopal Church, as mentioned above).

Diane Baptie has compiled an 81-page booklet, listing the *Registers of the Secession Churches in Scotland* with a cut-off point of 1900. The list covers the registers of the Reformed Presbyterian Church, the United Presbyterian Church and the Free Church that are held by the NRS (mainly in its CH3 collection) and by Scottish local archives.

The 68-page Spring/Summer 2004 issue of the British Isles Family History Society (BIFHS) USA's Journal (Volume XVII, No. 1) consists entirely of a list of *Scottish Nonconformist Church Records* compiled by Sam Gibson, a consultant and teacher of Scottish research at the Los Angeles LDS Family History Centre.

The listing (which includes many registers of the secession churches, the Roman Catholic Church and the 'Quakers', and some registers of the Scottish Episcopal Church, Methodist Church and other nonconformist churches) includes the NRS reference numbers. In addition, the call numbers of registers and indexes that have been microfilmed by the LDS Church are included. Such registers can be made available on loan from the LDS Family History Library in Salt Lake City to any of the worldwide LDS Family History Centres.

On the FamilySearch website **www.familysearch.org**, some of the records of these churches are included in the LDS International Genealogical Index (IGI) and its successor Scottish baptism and marriage databases.

There are two helpful websites that can tell you which churches are included in the IGI/FamilySearch databases. Hugh Wallis's IGI Batch Numbers site **http://freepages.genealogy.rootsweb.ancestry.com/~hughwallis/IGIBatchNumbers.htm#Menu** has been available for some time. It has recently been joined by a similar site created by Steve Archer named FamilySearch: a Guide to the British batches **www.archersoftware.co.uk/igi/index.htm**.

On both sites, you would click on 'Scotland', then on the name of the appropriate county (or, alternatively, on a county map on the Archer site), and look at the information for a particular parish, which you can then search. Steve Archer says that his site contains batches added to the IGI since 2002 that are not on the Wallis site.

You'll see, for example, that the baptisms of the Perth Associate Congregation are online from 1740-1854 and its marriages from 1740-1741 and 1778-1786. For the Leith Episcopal Congregation (of St. James's Church), however, baptisms are listed only from 1733-1775 and marriages only from 1738-1775, although more years are listed in D.J. Steel's list and that in the BIFHS Journal.

At the website of the Friends of Dundee City Archives **www.fdca.org.uk**, you'll find several family history databases, including Wesleyan Methodist baptisms 1765-1898, Hilltown Free Church baptisms 1846-1893, Dudhope Free Church admissions 1867-1874 and St. Peter's Free Church burials 1837-1846.

CHAPTER SEVEN

Wills and Inventories

As elsewhere, wills in Scotland are a very useful source of information about ancestors and relatives. Not everyone made a will, but if you can find one or more in your extended family, it can prove helpful in confirming relationships and filling in all sorts of details that you just don't get in the civil registration, census returns and church registers. The inventories that accompany the Scottish equivalents of wills and administrations can (if you're lucky) give you a remarkable view into the life of someone who may have lived several hundred years ago.

The court system dealing with testamentary records was quite different from that of England and Wales. The Scottish commissary courts had dealt with inheritance, and testaments in particular, from the middle of the 16th century up to the early 19th century. Their area of jurisdiction was called a commissariot, with boundaries corresponding to those of the medieval Scottish dioceses.

The commissary courts had taken over the functions of earlier church courts, with the establishment of the first such court in Edinburgh in 1564. (Unfortunately, the earlier records of Aberdeen Commissary Court were destroyed in a fire in 1721.)

From 1824, commissary courts ceased to have a separate existence and became a function of the already existing sheriff courts, which deal with both civil and criminal cases. This transfer was not immediate in all courts, and the Edinburgh Commissary Court (which dealt not only with the wills of people who died in the Edinburgh commissariot, but also of those who died elsewhere in the country, as well as people who died 'furth of Scotland') was the last to go in 1836.

The National Records of Scotland (NRS, formerly the National Archives of Scotland, and prior to that known as the Scottish Record Office) holds all the Scottish wills and inventories (strictly speaking, Scottish testamentary records) from the year 1513 up to a rolling cut-off point of ten years ago. For more recent records, you would need to contact the Commissary Department of Edinburgh Sheriff Court at 27 Chambers Street, Edinburgh EH1 1LB.

You can view the wills and inventories at the NRS free of charge, and they're online at the ScotlandsPeople website **www.scotlandspeople.gov.uk** up to 1901. Searching the index is free of charge, but viewing and downloading a document will cost you £5, no matter what its length is - and some can be more than 20 pages long.

Scotland has its own legal system, and the terminology used there is different to that of England and Wales. 'Testaments testamentar' are the Scottish equivalent of wills, and 'testaments dative' are the equivalent of letters of administration, dealing with the estates of those who died intestate in Scotland. These testaments are 'confirmed' rather than proved, so there's no such thing as probate in Scotland. Both types of testament generally include an inventory of the deceased person's moveable property.

This was divided into three parts under Scots law. One third would go to the widow (the 'jus relictae'), one third (or half, if their mother was already dead) divided equally between all the male and female children (the 'legitim' or 'bairns' pairt'), and the remaining third could go to whoever the deceased person wished to leave it to (and was therefore known as the 'deid's pairt').

Until the passage of the Heritable Jurisdictions Act in 1868, land and buildings could not be bequeathed via a testament testamentar, as they were 'heritable property', which passed to the eldest son automatically through the law of inheritance (see Chapter 13). The way round this was by a testator setting up a trust ('trust deed and settlement') during his or her lifetime, which would then carry out his or her wishes after death.

The following is an edited transcript of the testament testamentar of my 4X great-grandfather, Thomas Ritchie, a farmer in the parish of Aberdalgie, near Perth. I've divided the document into four parts and highlighted personal names in bold type.

Transcript of the testament testamentar and inventory of Thomas Ritchie
Reference CC7/9/2
Dunkeld Commissary Court, 1813

1. Introductory section

At Dunkeld the 31st day of May 1813, in presence of **Robert Stewart of Garth**, Commissary of the Commissariot of Dunkeld, compeared **Mr. John Leslie**, writer [to the signet = solicitor] in Dunkeld, as procurator for **George Ritchie** after-designed and gave in the Extract Registered Assignation by **Thomas Ritchie**, tenant in Aberdalgie, and inventory of his effects and oath thereon after-written, desiring the same might be registered in the Commissary Court Books of the Commissariot of Dunkeld conform to an Act of Parliament, which desire the said Commissary found reasonable and ordained the same to be done accordingly, whereof the tenor follows, vizt.

A testament always has an introductory clause, and it's worth persevering with the legalese in order to get to the more interesting parts of the testament.

2. The actual will

Now comes what in England would be considered the will itself, which is normally the second part of a testament testamentar, but wouldn't normally appear in a testament dative.

I, **Thomas Ritchie** tenant in Aberdalgie, for the love, favour and affection which I have and bear to **George Ritchie**, my only son; **Grizel Ritchie**, spouse of **James Lawson** of Easthaugh, my only surviving daughter; **May Craigie**, my spouse; and **Jean** and **May Morton**, daughters of the deceased **Andrew Morton**, her grandchildren; and for certain other causes and considerations me hereunto moving, do by these presents … assign and dispone to and in favour of the said **George Ritchie**, my only son and who succeeds me in my heritable property and his heirs and executors, all and whatsoever debts and sums of money heritable or moveable, gold, silver, coined and uncoined, goods, gear, lying money, bank notes, corn, cattle, instruments of husbandry, stocking and all other money and effects pertaining and belonging … to me at the time of my death, together with the bonds, bills, vouchers, obligations and all other rights and securities whatsoever, whether heritable or moveable, made, granted and conceived … in my favour … and to which I make the said **George Ritchie** … with full power after my death to enter into the possession of the same …

To the said **May Craigie**, my spouse, a free liferent annuity of £60 sterling during all the days of her life … and the use of my present dwelling-house during her life, and the subsistence of my tack [= lease] thereof,

To the said **Mrs. Grizel Lawson** in liferent during all the days of her lifetime and to **May Lawson** and **Elizabeth Lawson**, her daughters … the sum of £600 sterling.

To the said **Jean Morton** the sum of £100 sterling and to **May Morton** the sum of £110 sterling, and to each of them a chest of drawers and half a dozen of chairs of £10 value or thereby, with bedding for two beds out of my present house …

I do hereby legate and bequeath the household furniture of my present dwelling house … to the said **May Craigie** in liferent and thereafter to be equally divided between the said **George Ritchie** and **Mrs. Grizel Lawson**, only my son is to have my bureau or desk, and my said daughter her deceased sisters' drawers and chairs.

And further, I do hereby nominate and appoint the said **George Ritchie** to be my sole executor …

In witness whereof I have subscribed these presents written upon this and the two preceding pages of stamped paper by **Alexander Menzies**, apprentice to **William Ross**, writer in Perth, at Perth the 24th day of December 1802 … (signed) **Thomas Ritchie** …

3. Inventory

Inventory of the personal and moveable estate and effects which belonged to the deceased **Thomas Ritchie**, tenant in Aberdalgie, who died at Aberdalgie upon the (blank) day of December 1807, faithfully made and given up by **George Ritchie**, farmer at Cultmalundie, his only son and general disponee and sole executor …

Stocking of Aberdalgie

4 work horses at £20	£80	
4 cows at £8-8	£33-12/-	
4 two year olds at £6	£24	
4 one year olds at £3	£12	
4 calves at £1-10	£6	
		£155-12/-
Farm utensils	£40	
Crop on hand	£100	
Household furniture	£30	
		£170

Bill James Lawson principal	£600		
Interest 1 ½ years	£45		
		£645	
Bill Messrs. Buchan & Condie			
1 June 1804	£200		
Interest to Decr. 1807 from 22 May 7 months payable 22 May thereafter	£5-16/8		
		£205-16/8	
2 shares of the capital stock of the Perth Banking Company the input upon which was £100 each, and for which there was paid at winding up the concerns of the company £139 each	£278		
		£278	
			£1,454-8/8

4. Confirmatory section

At Perth the 7th day of May 1813, in presence of **Laurence Robertson**, Esqr., one of His Majesty's Justices of the Peace for the County of Perth and Commissioner appointed by the Commissary of Dunkeld, compeared **George Ritchie** of South Black Ruthven, residing at Cultmalundie, only lawful son of the deceased **Thomas Ritchie**, tenant in Aberdalgie, who being solemnly sworn and examined, depones that the said deceased **Thomas Ritchie**, his father, died upon the (blank) day of December 1807, that the deponent has entered upon the possession or management of the deceased's personal or moveable estate as sole executor nominated by his said father conform to Assignation or Deed of Settlement executed by him bearing the date 24th day of December 1802, that the deponent does not know of any settlement or writing relative to the disposal of the deceased's personal estate or effects … other than that now exhibited, that the preceding inventory … is a full and complete inventory of the personal estate and effects of the said deceased **Thomas Ritchie** wherever situated … and that the whole of the deceased's personal estate and effects situated in Scotland … is above the value of £1,000 sterling and under the value of £1,500 pounds sterling, all of which is truth as the deponent shall answer to God, (signed) **George Ritchie**, **Laur. Robertson J.P.**

This final section is the equivalent of a grant of probate in England and Wales. You'll notice that the testament was confirmed in May 1813, although Thomas Ritchie had died in December 1807. In the case of a dispute, or because of the death of an executor, a testament dative (and even a testament testamentar) could come before a court much later than you might expect. It's a good idea therefore to search for a testament for perhaps as much as 20 years after someone's death.

The will of Thomas Ritchie above is pretty straightforward. It states the family relationships and who's getting what, but it doesn't really tell you about the beneficiaries - or reveal anything about the testator. The following extracts from a 23-page will do that. In it, Thomas Ruthven, an Edinburgh solicitor, makes the sort of comments that it would be great to find in every will.

Thomas was the brother of my 5X great-grandmother, Eupham Ruthven. According to the record of his burial, Thomas had lived in Edinburgh at the foot of Carrubbers Close, one of the alleyways off the High Street, died of tuberculosis in April 1791 at the age of 51 and was buried in the graveyard of South Leith Church.

Partial transcript of the testament testamentar of Thomas Ruthven
Reference CC8/8/129
Edinburgh Commissary Court, 1793

> I, **Thomas Ruthven** writer in Edinburgh, ... having entire confidence in **Sir John Wishart Belsches of Fettercairn** who has been the best friend to me I ever had in the world, his friendship being all true and sincere, and who I know will condescend after my death to manage my funds to the best advantage for the behoof [= use] of those interested therein, though he is presently in the country during the vacation ...

According to the *Ordnance Gazetteer of Scotland*, Fettercairn in Kincardineshire had been held by the Middleton family for 500 years, but Sir John Wishart Belsches had bought the estate in 1777.

Thomas Ruthven was keen to make provision for his clerks, who appear in the will before anyone in his family.

> And [to pay] to **James Knox** my clerk who has been with me about 17 years and, except a few months at first, was alwise in family with me till his marriage in August 1788, with as much merit as perhaps any clerk ever had, besides his being a companion to me, as a friend in my house which I made him, much to my satisfaction, when I came to know him ... the sum of £400 sterling,

As also to **William Ellis** my other clerk … the sum of £100 sterling in token of my regard for him and entire approbation of him, who has been with me about four years immediately after his apprenticeship with much attachment to my person and interest.

And further, in case they my two clerks after my death shall carry on business for themselves in company, which is a plan I much approve of and wish them to follow, I authorise my said trustee … to make them a present of all my books, pamphlets and others of that kind, as also a present of all my writing desks, both in the writing room and my own business room, with all the seats and other things connected therewith, and my oval table for business in my said business room, and further, in the same event, I desire that they may have the use of my dwelling house to Whitsunday 1792 with all the furniture and everything else within the same …

And to provide for his servant:

To **Mary Haig**, my servant, who has been in my service about 16 years, an honest faithful servant and very useful to me all that time, and during all my distresses in point of my health which have now been for about two years and a half with variations without recovery, and particularly the first winter of my distress and this winter and spring when I was worst, she attended to me with as much knowledge, carefulness and comfort to me as perhaps a servant in her station did to a master, although this year she has not been in good health herself and is seemingly somewhat worn out in her constitution.

While she has through life saved none of her wages, but given all she could spare to her parents and other relations who were in straits during their lives, and since their deaths, she has not had time to save anything worthwhile except a few pounds … to the said **Mary Haig** an annuity of £12 sterling yearly during her life.

But without forgetting his relatives:

Further, as … my niece **Margaret Bayne** otherwise **Miller** and **David Miller**, baker in Perth, her husband, have after many years trial of their baker business, found it too hard on both their constitutions in the way they have always applied to it, it is therefore my wish and desire that, after my death, they should give up their said business as soon as convenient and go to and reside in the country. To induce them thereto, my said trustee … [is] to pay to the said **Margaret Miller** an annuity of £50 sterling yearly during her life, and to the said **David Miller**, in the event of his surviving her, an annuity of £25 sterling yearly during his life… But I recommend to them by no means to take a farm of any large extent, but a small moderate place …

> And further, my trustee is to pay to my sister's name daughter **Eupham Dick**, daughter of **James Dick** and **Ann Bayne** otherwise **Dick**, the sum of £300 sterling, and that at the first term of Whitsunday or Martinmas a year after her marriage.

Or the charities he supported:

> And further, as it is my wish that the charities about Edinburgh, which I contributed to while in life, should not be sufferers by my death, therefore I appoint my said trustee to pay to the Orphan Hospital of Edinburgh £50, to the Canongate Charity Workhouse £25, to the Society for Upholding an Evening Lecturer in Edinburgh … £25, and to the Dispensary at Edinburgh the like sum of £25, all sterling money …

However, this will also has a codicil:

> … in case **Eupham Dick** … shall not behave in every respect according to the wish and desire of … **Eupham Ruthven**, my sister and her grandmother, during all the days of my said sister's life, or even whatever the behaviour of the said **Eupham Dick** shall be, it shall in all events be in the power of the said **Eupham Ruthven** to deprive her, the said **Eupham Dick**, of all or any part of the provision of £300 sterling conceived in her favour by the said deed, and to take the whole or whatever part of the same she may think proper to herself or dispose thereof to any other person or persons she may incline.

I wonder what that was all about. It was probably fortunate for Eupham Dick (my 3X great-grandmother) that when Thomas Ruthven died, he hadn't signed the codicil! In 1794, a year after this will was confirmed, Eupham Dick married George Ritchie, the principal beneficiary of the previous will.

In the library of the Society of Genealogists

The Society's library contains nearly 30 indexes (published by the Scottish Record Society) of testaments confirmed in the Scottish commissary courts, as well as some indexes of inventories which largely finish in 1800. Indexes to the various commissariat courts after 1800 are available in the library on microfilm.

487	TAIT	JOHN SCOTT	22/11/1871	HOUSE PAINTER IN GLASGOW, SPOUSE OF JESSIE STARK OR TAIT	TRUST DISPOSITION AND DEED OF SETTLEMENT; CODICIL	GLASGOW SHERIFF COURT WILLS	SC36/51/60	VIEW (£5.00) (11 pages)
488	TAIT	JOHN SCOTT	22/11/1871	HOUSE PAINTER AT GLASGOW, BROTHER OF PETER TAIT	INVENTORY	GLASGOW SHERIFF COURT INVENTORIES	SC36/48/67	VIEW (£5.00) (7 pages)
489	TAIT	JOHN,	24/08/1871	TENANT OF LANGRIGG PARISH OF WHITSOME	I AND EXTRACT REGISTERED WILL AND TESTAMENT AND CODICIL	DUNS SHERIFF COURT INVENTORIES	SC60/41/24	VIEW (£5.00) (11 pages)
490	TAIT	JOHNE	01/06/1669	IN NETHERCRAIG, PARISH OF STRAITON	TD	GLASGOW COMMISSARY COURT	CC9/7/37	VIEW (£5.00) (2 pages)
491	TAIT	JOHNE	09/03/1668	TAILOR AT LONDON	TESTAMENT DATIVE AND INVENTORY	EDINBURGH COMMISSARY COURT	CC8/8/73	VIEW (£5.00) (3 pages)
492	TAIT	JOHNE	23/05/1671	MERCHANT, BURGESS OF EDINBURGH	TESTAMENT TESTAMENTAR AND INVENTORY	EDINBURGH COMMISSARY COURT	CC8/8/74	VIEW (£5.00) (8 pages)
493	TAIT	JOHNE	06/06/1663	AND MARGARET T., HIS SPOUSE, IN SAINT OLA, ORKNEY	TD	ORKNEY & SHETLAND COMMISSARY COURT	CC17/2/7	VIEW (£5.00) (2 pages)
494	TAIT	JOHNE	12/08/1633	IN DEWAR, PARISH OF HERIOTMURE, SHERIFFDOM OF EDINBURGH	TESTAMENT TESTAMENTAR AND INVENTORY	EDINBURGH COMMISSARY COURT	CC8/8/56	VIEW (£5.00) (2 pages)
495	TAIT	JOHNNE	24/05/1605	WILLIAM, AND BERNARD, LAWFUL SONS TO UMQUHILE T., PARISH OF RERIK, STEWARTRY OF KIRKCUDBRIGHT	TESTAMENT DATIVE AND INVENTORY	EDINBURGH COMMISSARY COURT	CC8/8/40	VIEW (£5.00) (1 pages)

9. Wills and testaments search returns.

364

and Sums of Money, which were addebted and resting owing to
Umquhile John Brodie residing in the Northgate of Peebles
at the time of his death, which happened at Peebles upon
the Twenty first day of November one thousand eight hundred
and thirty one, made and given up by the Defunct him-
-self upon the seventh day of the said Month of November
eighteen hundred and thirty one, in so far as Concerns the
nomination of his Executors, and now made and given
up by James Turnbull Joiner in Peebles and John
Fothringham Writer there in so far as Concerns the debts
specified in the Inventory after written, which James Turnbull
and John Fothringham the said Umquhile John Brodie
did nominate and appoint to be his sole executors
and universal intromitters with his estate and effects and
that by a Deed of Settlement executed by him on the
said Seventh day of November Eighteen hundred and
thirty one and recorded in the Books of Session at
Edinburgh the Eleventh day of September eighteen
hundred and thirty two, and also in the register
of Inventories for the Commissariot of Peebles the
seventeenth day of June eighteen hundred and thirty
four. The said Umquhile John Brodie had per-
-taining and belonging addebted, resting owing to him
at the time of his decease foresaid, the Goods and
Gear, debts Sums of Money and others Contained in
the Inventory of his personal Estate given in upon
oath by the said James Turnbulls and John
Fothringhams and recorded in the register of In-
-ventories for the Commissariot of Peebles on the
said Seventeenth day of June Eighteen hundred
and thirty four of which Inventory the tenor follows
Vizt

1 Book debts due by Sundries supposed recoverable Viz

	£	s	d
By Mr James Spalding Nurseryman Peebles	19	14	-
Mr James Eckford Traquair mill	2	6	8
Carried forward	£22	-	8½

10. *Testament testamentar of John Brodie, confirmed in 1836.*

365

	£	s	d	£	s	d
Brought forward £				22	.	8½
By Mr Robert Brodie, Smith Templebar				10	14	.
Mr John Wilson formerly Writer in Peebles now in Edinburgh				24	10	.
Mr Alexander Murray Bartram Writer Peebles				12	.	.
Mr David Noble Attestone				7	9	.
£				76	13	8½
2 Books Debts due by Sundries but desperate from the Circumstances of the debtors Vizt						
By James Ker Writer Peebles £	4					
Mr John Forsyth Roads	3	3	2½			
William Young Carter Peebles	3	.	5			
William Ballantyne Eddlestone mill	3	18	.			
William Fairgrieve Carter Peebles	3	4	.			
William Burnett Saddler Peebles	11	8	8			
Thomas Granger ^ Peebles (margin: ^ Brewer)	73					
James White joiner Peebles	37	.	4½			
£	138	14	8			

Upon which no value whatever can be put, Some of the debtors being dead, and the others utterly insolvent.

	£	s	d	£	s	d
3 Bills due by sundries but desperate. Principal bill dated 14th February 1818 drawn by the deceased upon and accepted by Walter Laidlaw formerly at Glenrath now in America payable six months after date £	50					
Interest thereof from 14 February 1832	24	8	4			
Principal sum Contained in Bill dated 13 November 1812 drawn by the deceased upon and accepted by John Forsyth Farmer Roads now deceased payable 12 Months after date	50					
Interest thereof from 12 November 1823	20	1	1			
Principal Sum Contained in Bill dated 25th August 1814 drawn by the deceased						
Carried forward £	144	9	5½	76	13	8½

upon

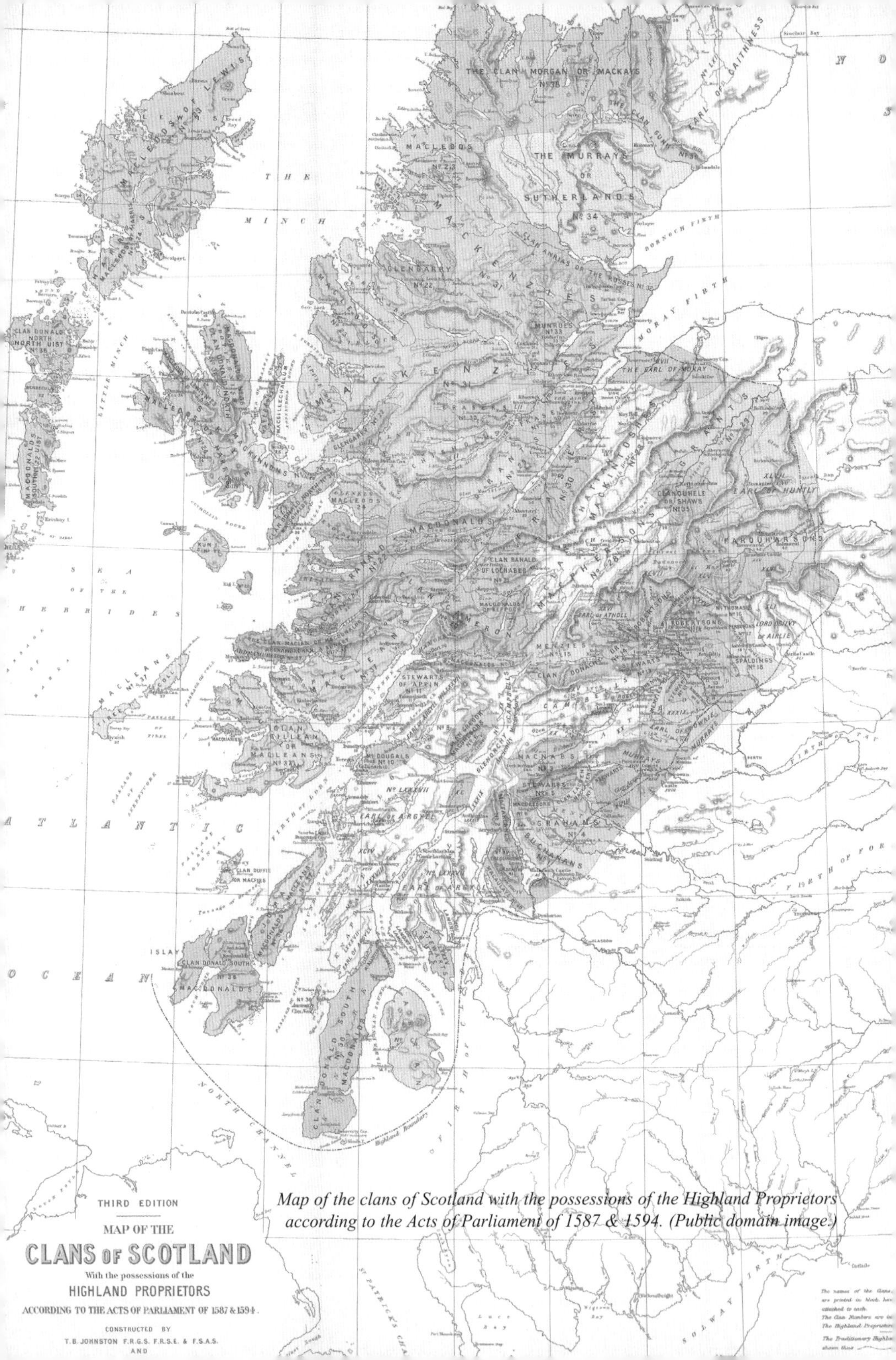

Map of the clans of Scotland with the possessions of the Highland Proprietors according to the Acts of Parliament of 1587 & 1594. (Public domain image.)

CHAPTER EIGHT

Scottish Clans and Families

A clan is basically an extended family: the word comes from the Gaelic *clann*, meaning 'children'. This is why many of the clan surnames are prefixed with 'Mac' or 'Mc', meaning 'son of'. Duncan Forbes of Culloden, Lord President of the Court of Session (Scotland's supreme civil court) wrote that a clan was a group of people with the same surname, who believed they were related to each other and had the same ancestry.

A clan might consist of several sub-groups, each with its own chieftain, but they would all owe allegiance to the main clan chief and saw it as their duty to support him in all his 'adventures'.

Forbes was writing about Highland clans in 1746 (at the time of the last Jacobite rebellion). If he had been writing 200 years earlier, he could just as easily have been describing the large family groups of the Scottish Borders, who also supported their chiefs in their adventures as 'reivers' (livestock raiders).

The people who made up the majority of the Highland clansmen and -women were a mixture of the descendants of the:

- **Picts**, north-east of the Forth and Clyde from late Roman times;
- **Scots**, in Argyll from the fifth century at the latest (but who may have arrived in the western Highlands and islands much earlier than that);
- **Vikings** from Norway, ruling over most of the Highlands and Western Isles for nearly 400 years until 1266 - and Orkney and Shetland for a further 200.

Were the people of a clan really related to each other? Duncan Forbes wrote that they 'believed' they were. The *chiefs* of several clans had continental origins, however: the Chisholm, Fraser, Gordon, Lindsay and Sinclair chiefs were of Norman or French origin, the Murray and Sutherland chiefs were said to be of Flemish descent, the Leslie chief Hungarian, and the chiefs of the Stewarts were Breton.

Because the chiefly families had these origins, it doesn't necessarily mean that their clanspeople did. Indeed, George F. Black, in *The Surnames of Scotland*, gives a number of examples of Highlanders taking on the name of a chief whose protection they wanted. According to Black, many people took on the surname Campbell in Argyll, MacDonald in the Western Isles and Kintyre, MacKenzie in Wester Ross, and Gordon in Strathbogie in Aberdeenshire. There were also Bissetts who became Frasers, as well as some people baptised as 'Cumins of the hen-trough'.

Some protected families became 'septs' (associated families) of a clan, although most septs were families who descended from a clan chief, but used a different surname. An example of this is the various Caithness families descended from Clan Gunn (of Norse origin): the Georgesons (descended from George Gunn), Hendersons (from Henry), Jamesons (James), Johnsons (John), Mansons (Magnus), Nelsons (Neil), Robsons (Robert), Sandisons (Alexander), Swansons (Sweyn), Williamsons and Wilsons (from two different Williams).

Sir Thomas Innes of Learney, a former Lord Lyon King of Arms, considered that almost all Scots were 'in some line of ancestry' connected to Fergus Mor MacEarc, King of Scots in the fifth century and ancestor of the present Queen. Likewise, the genealogist and herald Sir Iain Moncreiffe wrote that there was a strong likelihood by the 19th century of any MacKay clansman in Sutherland or any Robertson in Perthshire being descended from King Robert the Bruce, who reigned in the early 14th century.

This, said Sir Iain, was through the marriages of the granddaughters of Bruce's grandson Robert II (the first of the Stewart kings of Scotland) to clan chiefs, followed by 500 years of intermarriage down through the levels of clan society. This would also apply to the men and women of various other clan names, such as Campbell, Forbes, MacDonald, MacKenzie and Stewart of Appin. The Stewarts in

Atholl, however, are said to be descended from the illegitimate children of Alexander Stewart, Earl of Buchan and Badenoch, a wild and warlike son of Robert II and known as the 'Wolf of Badenoch'.

After the defeat of 'Bonnie Prince Charlie's rebellion at the Battle of Culloden in 1746, the British Government tried to destroy the clan system by confiscating Jacobite chiefs' estates, prohibiting Highlanders from carrying weapons, and removing the chiefs' right to hold courts of law. Wearing tartan was banned until 1782, with the result that most of the old patterns were lost and today's tartans were almost all created after that date. You can view thousands of tartan designs at the website of the Scottish Register of Tartans **www.tartanregister.gov.uk**.

Many Highlanders emigrated to North America, and later to Australia and New Zealand. At first, the move was voluntary, but the late 18th and 19th centuries saw many clan lands turned over to sheep farming in the notorious 'Highland Clearances'. Absentee chiefs and lowland factors drove out the Gaelic-speaking natives, so that they could 'improve' their lands. The county of Sutherland was a particularly bad case, where many tenants were evicted by force and their homes destroyed in the name of progress.

Clans began to come in from the cold with the formation of clan societies (the earliest of which dated back to the early 18th century). Sir Walter Scott was largely responsible for restoring Highland clans and tartans to an important position through organising a gathering of the clans in 1822 at which the guest of honour was no less than King George IV himself.

More recently, in July 2009, Prince Charles (the Duke of Rothesay, when in Scotland) attended the largest-ever international gathering of the clans in Edinburgh, as part of the Homecoming celebrations. Unfortunately, although the event was considered a success, it lost money and will not be repeated in Edinburgh at the 2014 Homecoming. Something along those lines may take place as part of the celebration of the 700th anniversary of the Battle of Bannockburn (also in 2014).

Many of the modern-day clans are participating in the Scottish DNA Project **www.scottishdna.net**, which aims to provide DNA information for all clans and families of Scottish ancestry. Ideally, a man's Y-DNA signature (the genetic make-up of his Y-chromosome, which is passed from father to son with occasional minor mutations) would indicate which clan or family he belongs to.

Alistair McIntyre's website Electric Scotland has a great deal of information on Scottish and Irish clans and families at **www.electricscotland.com/webclans**. The site includes a clan map published in 1899 by W. & A.K Johnston (showing the clan lands in the late 16th century), which you can download in a high definition format (illustrated on page 62). There are also web pages with information for about 270 Scottish surnames, including PDF versions of many 19th century books, as well as links to clan societies and other relevant websites.

Scottish heraldry

Heraldry in Scotland is the responsibility of the Lord Lyon King of Arms and his heraldic court in New Register House, Edinburgh. You can read about the work of the Lyon Court at its website **www.lyon-court.com**, which contains photographs of the Lord Lyon and his Officers of Arms wearing their colourful tabards bearing the royal arms, as well as information about coats of arms, Scottish clans and tartans, and flying flags.

A coat of arms is particular to one individual and, in Scotland, using unauthorised arms is a criminal offence which the Lord Lyon can prosecute under a 1592 Act of the Scottish Parliament. If you wish to have your own coat of arms, you can apply by petitioning the Lord Lyon for a Grant of Arms (costing either £1,364 for a shield with or without motto, or £2,106 for a shield and crest with or without motto) or a 'matriculation' (at a considerably lower cost) if you can trace your line back to an ancestor with the same surname who had a Grant of Arms.

The new arms are entered in the Public Register of All Arms and Bearings in Scotland, which may be inspected for a fee at New Register House. You can search the register from its first entries in 1672 up to 1908 free of charge at the ScotlandsPeople website **www.scotlandspeople.gov.uk**. The entries from 1672-1804 are brief with very little family history information and few images of the coats of arms.

You can read more about Scottish coats of arms at the website of the Heraldry Society of Scotland **www.heraldry-scotland.co.uk**, which was founded in 1977. The society's site contains many full-colour illustrations of coats of arms, grants and matriculations, and other heraldic designs.

Histories of Scottish families

Many books have been written about Scottish clans and families. Particularly good examples of the books covering many families are:

1. Frank Adam's *The Clans, Septs and Regiments of the Scottish Highlands*;
2. *The Tartans of the Clans and Families of Scotland* by Sir Thomas Innes of Learney (a former Lord Lyon);
3. Sir Iain Moncreiffe of that Ilk's *The Highland Clans* (which has endpapers showing the descent of the Scottish clans from Irish and Norse royalty);
4. The *Scottish Clan and Family Encyclopedia* by George Way of Plean and Romilly Squire.

The second and fourth books cover not only Highland clans, but also Lowland and Border families, while the first has very good information about the septs of the Highland clans. The late Sir Iain Moncreiffe's book is written in his usual idiosynchratic style.

To find printed histories of individual families, you should refer to Joan PS Ferguson's *Scottish Family Histories*, which lists all those available in Scottish libraries, including the National Library of Scotland.

The Oxford Dictionary of National Biography (DNB) includes the biographies of around 6,000 people born in Scotland or who lived there, covering the last 1,500 years. You can take out a personal subscription to the DNB at **www.oup.com/oxforddnb/info/subscribe**, but you may find that your local library service has already subscribed and that you can use their subscription from home. The subscription website Ancestry.co.uk **www.ancestry.co.uk** has a searchable version of the 1921-22 issue of the DNB (minus one of its 22 volumes).

Peerage and landed gentry

You may be fortunate enough to find a 'gateway' ancestor in your research, who will open the door to a vast world of research that's already been carried out into the genealogy of the landed gentry, the peerage and even royalty. Your humble ancestors may be descended (perhaps, like mine, illegitimately) from a family that owned property (in my case, the Ritchies in the south of Perthshire).

That family may be descended from a wealthier gentry family, some of whom were 'lairds' (lords of the manor) and whose genealogy is recorded in volumes such as *Burke's Landed Gentry* (in my case, this family was the Ruthvens). In the ancestry of the gentry family, you're quite likely to find noble predecessors whose marriages may lead you to the Kings of Scotland. (The Ruthvens of Freeland - who I *may* be related to - were descended from the second Lord Ruthven, who married Lady Dirleton, a descendant of King Robert the Bruce.)

There are many peerage guides, including *The Complete Peerage* (in 14 volumes), *The Peerage of Scotland*, *Burke's Peerage* and *Debrett's Peerage*. The most recent volume of *Burke's Landed Gentry: The Kingdom in Scotland* includes the Scottish peerage and clan chiefs. You can read a number of these books online at the Internet Archive **http://archive.org** or at Google Books **http://books.google.co.uk**.

You can subscribe to Burke's Peerage and Gentry information online at **www.burkespeerage.com**, where you can view the royal lineage (including the Scottish kings from the union of the Picts and Scots in 844) free of charge. *Debrett's Peerage and Baronetage* is also available online as a digital subscription at **www.exacteditions.com**. Also very useful is Darryl Lundy's free website The Peerage **www.thepeerage.com**.

In the library of the Society of Genealogists

The Society's library holds the above-mentioned books on clan and family surnames (as well as Sir Thomas Innes's *Scots Heraldry* and Margaret Stuart's *Scottish Family History*, which lists books and articles on individual families) on the Scottish shelves of its Middle Library. In addition, you'll find peerage and landed gentry directories in the Upper Library, as well as histories of individual families.

CHAPTER NINE
Records of the Armed Forces

1. British Army

Other ranks

According to John Sadler's *Scottish Battles*, more than half a million Scots enlisted to fight in the First World War, representing almost a quarter of the male population and half of those aged 15-49. Scots have traditionally made a significant contribution to the British Army.

Records for Scots in the armed forces since the union with England and Wales in 1707 are held by The National Archives (TNA) in Kew, London, and many of the records are available online. TNA has a large number of detailed research guides to these records at **www.nationalarchives.gov.uk/records/research-guide-listing.htm**. In addition, the National Army Museum in London has useful information on tracing your ancestors' military careers at **www.nam.ac.uk/research/family-history**.

There are different British Army records for officers and the so-called 'other ranks' (privates and non-commissioned officers). For the period prior to the First World War, the service records for other ranks are in TNA's incomplete WO (War Office) 97 collection. These records, covering soldiers discharged to pension between 1760 and 1913, have been digitised and indexed, and

are available online at the subscription/pay-per-view site Findmypast **www.findmypast.co.uk**.

More service records for soldiers discharged to pension between 1787 and 1813 are held in the WO 121 collection. These records have not been digitised, but are indexed in the TNA Catalogue **www.nationalarchives.gov.uk/catalogue**. The results of a search will give you information, such as:

> WO 121/155/164 - Duncan Campbell; born in Cregnish, Argyll; served in 74th Foot Regiment, and Argyllshire Fencibles; discharged in 1802 aged 42, after 11 years 6 months service.

Having found the appropriate reference number, you can then order the record from TNA.

As well as service records, TNA also holds muster rolls and pay lists for other ranks, which state enlistment dates, movements and discharge dates. Monthly or quarterly musters (which were used for pay and accounting) usually give the age, place of enlistment and trade in a recruit's first entry.

Muster rolls and pay lists for most regiments from 1730-1878 are in the series WO 12, while those for the Artillery are in WO 10, WO 54 and WO 69, for the Engineers in WO 11 and WO 54, for militia and volunteers in WO 13 and WO 68, and for troops sent to the Scutari Depot during the Crimean War from 1854-56 are in WO 14. The 1861 Worldwide Army Index at Findmypast contains information from the WO 10, WO 11 and WO 12 collections.

As well as the WO 97 and WO 121 soldiers' pension records, the WO 116 collection contains disability pension admission books from 1715-1882, while length of service books from 1823-1913 are in the WO 117 collection. Both WO 116 and WO 117 records can be downloaded (currently free of charge) as a large block of unindexed 'digital microfilm' from TNA's Documents Online website **www.nationalarchives.gov.uk/documentsonline**.

For the First World War period, about 60% of the records of the other ranks were unfortunately destroyed by enemy bombing in 1940, including the records of soldiers who had enlisted prior to the war, and were still in service or recalled to it. However, the records for around two million soldiers either survived and are in the WO 363 collection (these are known as the 'burnt documents'), or they were reconstructed from pension records and are in the WO 364 collection.

Both of these collections have been digitised and indexed, and are available online at the subscription website Ancestry.co.uk **www.ancestry.co.uk**. In these collections, you'll also find the service records of soldiers such as my grandfather, John MacKenzie, who served in the Royal Scots for 21 years from 1889-1910 and then in the Labour Corps and the Military Police from 1914-1919 (and also the earlier service records of a few soldiers who didn't serve during the First World War).

Officers

Printed records of British Army officers are contained in the official *Army List*, first published in 1740, and in the unofficial *Hart's Army List*, published from 1839-1915. Many of these lists have been digitised and can be viewed online at the subscription/pay-per-view site The Genealogist **www.thegenealogist.co.uk** and free of charge at the Internet Archive **www.archive.org**.

In addition, you can download both the TNA collections WO 65 (Printed Annual Army Lists) and WO 76 (Records of Officers' Service) as a large block of 'digital microfilm' from Documents Online. Digital microfilm is currently free of charge.

The main series of officers' service records for the First World War years was destroyed in 1940, just like the other ranks' records. However, there is still a supplementary series of records for officers, although unfortunately some had been destroyed by clerks. In some cases, the records contain attestation papers, service record and personal correspondence, but in others, there's only the date of the officer's death.

In the WO 339 collection, you'll find nearly 140,000 service records of officers who were either a regular Army officer before the First World War, given a temporary commission or commissioned into the Special Reserve of officers. In addition, the WO 374 collection contains almost 80,000 records of officers with a Territorial Army or temporary commission. You can search for both WO 339 and WO 374 records in TNA's Catalogue.

British Army records online

Ancestry.co.uk (A) **www.ancestry.co.uk**

- British Army World War I Service Records 1914-1920 (TNA ref. WO 363).
- British Army World War I Pension Records 1914-1920 (WO 364).
- British Army World War I Medal Rolls Index Cards 1914-1920 (WO 372) (Also DO).

- Royal Naval Division Casualties of the Great War 1914-1924.
- Army War List 1893.
- Military Campaign Medal and Award Rolls 1793-1949 (WO 100).
- Indian Army Quarterly List 1912.
- Perthshire Militia Survey 1802.
- Kirkcaldy and District War Album - photographs of more than 200 Fife men serving in South Africa, from the *Fifeshire Advertiser* 1900-1902.

Findmypast (FMP) **www.findmypast.co.uk**

- British Army Service Records 1760-1913 (WO 97)
- Militia Service Records 1806-1915 (WO 96)
- 1861 Worldwide Army Index (WO 10, WO 11, WO 12)
- Army Deserters 1828-1840
- Other Army Lists and Roll Calls (includes Grenadier Guards 1656-1874; Peninsular Medal Roll 1793-1814; Waterloo Roll Call 1815; Army Lists 1787, 1798 and 1878; Hart's Army List 1840 and 1888; and Indian Army and Civil Service List 1873)
- Royal Fusiliers Collection 1863-1905
- Royal Naval Division 1914-1919
- Armed Forces Births 1761-2005, Marriages 1796-2005 and Deaths 1796-2005

Military Genealogy (MG) **www.military-genealogy.com**

- Soldiers Died in the Great War 1914-1919 (Also A, FMP)
- National Roll of the Great War 1914-1918 (Also A, FMP, TG)
- De Ruvigny's Roll of Honour 1914-1924 (Also A, FMP, TG)
- Citations of the Distinguished Conduct Medal 1914-1920 (Also A, FMP)
- Army Roll of Honour 1939-1945 (Also A, FMP)
- British Army Prisoners of War 1939-1945 (Also A, FMP)
- Casualties of the Boer War 1899-1902 (Also A, FMP)
- Waterloo Medal Roll 1815 (Also A, FMP)

The Genealogist (TG) **www.thegenealogist.co.uk**

- Bond of Sacrifice officers' roll of honour August 1914-June 1915
- British Roll of Honour 1914-1918
- Chatham, Plymouth and Portsmouth Memorial Register 1914-1921
- Various regimental histories

Commonwealth War Graves Commission (CWGC) **www.cwgc.org**

- Debt of Honour Register (for First and Second World Wars)

Documents Online (DO) **www.nationalarchives.gov.uk/documentsonline**

- Selected First World War and Army of Occupation War Diaries (WO 95)
- Women's (later Queen Mary's) Army Auxiliary Corps 1917-1920 (WO 398)
- British prisoners of war: interviews and reports (WO 161)
- Victoria Cross Registers (WO 98) (Also A)
- Recommendations for Honours and Awards 1935 - 1990 (WO 373)

Other Boer War databases

- Roll of Honour **www.roll-of-honour.com/Databases/BoerDetailed/index.html**
- Casus Belli **www.casus-belli.co.uk**

2. Royal Navy

Ratings

In the Royal Navy, ordinary seamen (the equivalent of 'other ranks' in the British Army), are known as 'ratings'. There are Continuous Service Engagement Books for ratings joining the Navy from 1853-72 in the TNA collection ADM (Admiralty) 139. Those joining from 1873-1923 are included in the Register of Seamen's Services in ADM 188. Both of these collections are now searchable online at Documents Online (see below).

If you have an ancestor who fought with Lord Nelson in the Battle of Trafalgar in 1805, you should be able to find him in TNA's Trafalgar ancestors database (of over 8,000 mainly Royal Navy and Royal Marines personnel) at **www.nationalarchives.gov.uk/trafalgarancestors**.

Officers

There were registers of officers' services from 1756-1966, although most cover the period 1840-1920. These records make up the series ADM 196, which has been digitised and can be searched at Documents Online (see below).

For earlier officers' service, you should look in the unofficial *Steele's Navy List*, which was published from 1782, the official *Navy List*, published quarterly from

1814, and the unofficial *New Navy List* (which contains short biographies), published from 1841-56. As with the *Army List*, digitised copies of the various *Navy List* versions are accessible online at The Genealogist and at the Internet Archive.

Royal Navy records online

Documents Online

- Register of Seamen's Services 1853-1923 (ADM 139, ADM 188)
- Royal Naval Officers' Service Records 1756-1917 (ADM 196)
- Royal Naval Officers' Service Record Cards and Files 1880-1960 (ADM 340)
- Royal Naval Division Service Records 1914-1919 (ADM 339)
- Royal Naval Volunteer Reserve, First World War (ADM 337)
- Royal Naval Reserve Service Records 1860-1908 (BT 164)
- Women's Royal Naval Service 1917-1919 (ADM 318, ADM 336)
- Wills of Royal Naval Seamen 1786-1882 (ADM 48)

Ancestry.co.uk

- British Naval Biographical Dictionary 1849
- Commissioned Sea Officers of the Royal Navy 1660-1815
- Royal Navy and Royal Marine War Graves Roll 1914-1919
- Navy Medal and Award Rolls 1793-1972

Findmypast

- Royal Naval Officers 1914-1920 (ADM 171/89-93, ADM 171/139)

Military Genealogy

- Naval Casualties 1914-1919 (Also FMP, and similar to Ancestry's Royal Naval Division Casualties)

3. Royal Air Force

Airmen

The Royal Air Force (RAF) didn't exist until 1 April 1918, when the Royal Flying Corps (RFC, which was an Army unit that had been set up in 1912) was combined with the Royal Naval Air Service (RNAS, which had been founded in 1914), and began taking on new recruits.

‘Airmen’ are the equivalent in the RAF of ‘other ranks’ in the British Army. For the records of airmen who died or were discharged before the formation of the RAF, you’ll find the RFC service records in the WO 363 or 364 collections (online at Ancestry.co.uk), and the RNAS service records in ADM 188 (at Documents Online).

The RFC or RNAS records of airmen who were still serving when the RAF was created were transferred to the new service. These records, together with those of airmen who joined up after the creation of the RAF, are in the series AIR 79, with an index in AIR 78. These records are not yet available online.

Officers

You can find service records of RAF and RFC officers in the TNA collection AIR 76, which you’ll find at Documents Online. AIR 76 also holds records of officers of the RNAS who were still serving when the RAF was founded, while the records of those officers who had died or been discharged before 1918 are in the ADM 273 collection, which you can search in TNA’s Catalogue. You can also find RAF officers in the official *Air Force List* from March 1919. The 1939 list is available online at The Genealogist.

Royal Air Force records online

Documents Online

- RAF Officers’ Service Records 1918-1919 (AIR 76)
- WRAF Service Records 1918-1920 (AIR 80)
- Air Combat Reports, Second World War (AIR 50)

4. Royal Marines

Other ranks

First raised in 1664, the Royal Marines (RM) are ‘sea soldiers’ and are neither part of the British Army nor of the Royal Navy. TNA holds their attestation forms (enlistment and discharge papers) from 1790-1925 in its ADM 157 collection, which is being indexed in the TNA Catalogue.

In addition, there are description books from 1755-1940 in ADM 158, and service records from 1842-1936 in ADM 159, which have been digitised and indexed, and made available online at TNA’s Documents Online website.

The main divisions of the RM were based in the southern English ports of Chatham (in Kent), Portsmouth (Hampshire), Plymouth (Devon) and from 1805-69 Woolwich (Kent, and now the London Borough of Greenwich). The TNA records also cover the RM Artillery, RM Engineers and RM Labour Corps (in Chatham and Deal).

Officers

RM officers are listed in the *Army List* from 1740, the *Navy List* from 1797, *Hart's Army List* and the *New Navy List* from 1840, many editions of which you'll find online at the Internet Archive. RM officers' service records (from 1793 onwards) are held with those of Royal Navy officers in TNA's ADM 196 collection, which you can find at Documents Online.

Royal Marines' records online

Documents Online

- Royal Marines Registers of Service 1842-1936 (ADM 159)
- Selected Plymouth Attestations 1805-1848 (ADM 157/140)

Ancestry.co.uk

- Royal Navy and Royal Marine War Graves Roll 1914-1919

Findmypast

- Royal Marine Medal Roll 1914-1920 (ADM 171/167-171, ADM 171/92, ADM 171/139)

Applying for a post-First World War serviceman's record

The Ministry of Defence (MOD, the successor to the War Office) holds the records of British Army other ranks still serving in the Army after 1920 and officers still serving after 31 March 1922.

In addition, the MOD holds the records of ratings who joined the Royal Navy after 1923 and those already serving who served beyond 1928, as well as those of officers serving after the First World War.

The Ministry has records of airmen whose service number is higher than 329000 (and also of those whose number is lower, but served in the RAF during the Second World War), and of officers still serving after 1920.

Records of Royal Marines other ranks who enlisted after 1925 are also held by the MOD, as are those of officers who were appointed after that year.

You can apply to the MOD for information from the record of someone who served in the forces - and whose service record has not yet been made available at The National Archives. You'll need to supply the person's death certificate and pay a fee of £30. There's a link to the MOD website, which has full information and downloadable application forms, at **www.veterans-uk.info/service_records/service_records.html**

1799 map of Scotland by the English map publisher Clement Cruttwell. (Public domain image.)

CHAPTER TEN
Scottish Maps

The National Library of Scotland (NLS) has made more than 20,000 maps of Scotland available online free of charge at **http://maps.nls.uk**. The earliest map in the collection is Italian, made by Paolo Forlani between 1558 and 1566 and covers the whole of Scotland. The most recent are Ordnance Survey Air Photo Mosaics of Scotland published from 1944-1950.

The county maps are useful for family historians, and you can select them from a list of county names or by clicking on the relevant county on maps of north or south Scotland. The Ordnance Survey One-inch map second edition 1898-1904 is particularly helpful, as the parishes are shown in different colours. You can enlarge the maps on screen so that you can see a high level of detail.

Beware, however, as there were many parish and county boundary changes in 1891 (see below), so you may need to look at earlier maps too.

Also helpful for genealogy are the Ordnance Survey large-scale town plans published between 1847 and 1895 that are also available to view at the site.

Again, you can select a plan from a map of Scotland or from a list of nearly 80 plans (including Berwick-upon-Tweed). Both the town plans and county maps can be viewed as overlays to Google's maps.

In addition, the NLS map site has marine charts, military maps, a survey of fresh-water lochs, and a small number of estate maps from 1772-1878. There are ten estate maps for Edinburgh and two for Sutherland (farms in Golspie and Loth parishes c.1772 and Assynt in 1774).

Another free website that has photographs, maps and other useful information about parishes is ScotlandsPlaces **www.scotlandsplaces.gov.uk**. You can select a pre-1975 county from a list or map of Scotland to get information on a county-wide basis, and then narrow it down to local level by selecting a parish from a county map.

The site also has digitised images of the schedules of the Farm Horse Tax of 1797-1798, which names all those people who owned farm horses, parish-by-parish (except Inverness-shire, for which the figures are not divided by parish). The schedules act as a heads-of-household census substitute for the end of the 18th century.

You may also be able to find family members in the report of the Land Ownership Commission of 1872-1873, which lists all owners of one acre or more of land.

In addition, the site has information on the late 19th century boundary changes mentioned above, which are detailed in *Boundaries of Counties and Parishes in Scotland: as settled by the Boundary Commissioners under the Local Government (Scotland) Act, 1889*.

There are also Medical Officer of Health reports from 1891 for all counties except Bute, Kincardineshire, Kinross-shire, Orkney and Shetland, while the report for Perthshire covers the period 1891-1897. The reports contain information on sanitary improvements required and epidemics, with tables of births and deaths (showing numbers within certain age groups and numbers dying from eight specified diseases) for all parishes within a county.

CHAPTER ELEVEN
Scottish Newspapers

Civil registration certificates, census returns and parish registers provide the basic information that you need to build your family tree. Wills can provide more detail, but you may find that you still have only a basic skeleton for your family story. Looking at old newspapers can be a great help in finding the flesh to put on the bare bones.

Probably the earliest Scottish newspaper was the *Mercurius Caledonius*, published in Edinburgh in 1660 (although there had been earlier publications in Scotland reprinting London news). In the 18th century, the main newspapers in Scotland were the *Caledonian Mercury* (which was published between 1720 and 1867, *Edinburgh Evening Courant* 1718-1886 and *Edinburgh Advertiser* 1764-1859.

The Aberdeen-based *Press and Journal* (first published in 1747 as *Aberdeen's Journal*) was the first of today's Scottish newspapers to appear. It was followed in 1783 by the *Glasgow Advertiser*, which became the *Glasgow Herald* in 1805 and simply *The Herald* in 1992.

The Scotsman in Edinburgh, *The Courier* in Dundee (as the *Dundee Courier*) and the *Inverness Courier* were first published in 1817, followed by the *Perthshire Advertiser* in 1829, *Stirling Observer* in 1836, *Falkirk Herald* in 1845 and *Southern Reporter* in Selkirk in 1855.

You can find information on newspaper collections, with dates of publication, in Joan P.S. Ferguson's *Directory of Scottish Newspapers*. The directory lists newspapers held in 57 Scottish libraries (including public libraries, university libraries and the NLS), the British Library's Newspaper Library in London and Yale University Library in the United States, as well as those in newspaper publishers' offices.

At **www.nls.uk/collections/newspapers/indexes/index.cfm,** you'll find the NLS's free online Guide to Scottish Newspaper Indexes. The website Am Baile ('The Village') has free indexes to the *Inverness Journal* (1807-1849), *Inverness Advertiser* (1849-1885), *Inverness Courier* (1879, 1898-1901 and 1920-1939), *Scottish Highlander* (1885-1898), *John O'Groat Journal* (1836-1887) and *Gairm* (1952-2002) at **www.ambaile.org.uk/en/newspapers/index.jsp**.

You can search *The Scotsman*'s Digital Archive (1817-1950) free of charge at **http://archive.scotsman.com**. Viewing images of the newspaper costs from £7.95 for a 24-hour pass up to £159.95 for a year.

You'll find digitised copies of many British newspapers including the *Aberdeen Journal*, *Caledonian Mercury* and *Glasgow Herald* at the British Library's 19th Century Newspaper Collection **http://newspapers.bl.uk/blcs**. It'll cost you £6.99 for 24 hours (for up to 100 downloads) or £9.99 for seven days (and up to 200 downloads).

The subscription website **www.ancestry.co.uk** includes digitised images from several Scottish newspapers, including the *Dunfermline Journal*, *Edinburgh Evening Courant*, *Edinburgh Advertiser* and *Edinburgh Weekly Journal*.

The official Government journal, the *Edinburgh Gazette*, first published in 1699, has been digitised and is online free of charge at **www.edinburgh-gazette.co.uk**

The NLS has made available about 1,800 'broadsides' (single newssheets) published between 1650 and 1910 at **http://digital.nls.uk/broadsides**, where you can view them free of charge.

You can find links to today's Scottish national and local newspapers online at **www.onlinenewspapers.com/scotland.htm**.

Although your ancestor may never have left Scotland, it's worth searching the newspapers of Australia, New Zealand, etc., as they often reprinted unusual news items from the United Kingdom.

The commercial family history company brightsolid is digitising the British Library's collection of UK newspapers, formerly held at the Newspaper Library in Colindale, north London. The digitised images containing several Scottish papers are available online at the British Newspaper Archive website **www.britishnewspaperarchive.co.uk**.

You can buy limited access packages costing from £6.95 for two days (with 500 credits) to £29.95 for 30 days (with 3,000 credits). Searching the site is free of charge, but viewing a scanned page costs five credits (if the page was published more than 107 years ago and scanned from microfilm in black and white), 10 credits (if over 107 years old and scanned in colour) and 15 credits (if less than 107 years old and scanned in colour). You can also buy a year's unlimited access for £79.95.

Castle Street and municipal buildings, Aberdeen, Scotland between 1890 and 1905.
(Public domain image.)

CHAPTER TWELVE

Statistical Accounts of Scotland

The first volume of the first Statistical Account of Scotland was published in 1791. A year earlier, Sir John Sinclair, the MP for Caithness, had persuaded the 938 ministers of the Church of Scotland to write what he termed 'statistical accounts' of their parishes.

To assist the ministers, Sir John had sent them 160 questions: 40 on the geography and topography of the parish, 60 on its population, 16 on agriculture and 44 on general topics like the cost of living. Although some of the clergymen needed reminding (and Sir John ended up writing some accounts himself), the vast majority wrote accounts that Sir John published in 21 volumes between 1791 and 1799.

Sir John explained in his introduction that his original intention had been merely to compile a general statistical report about Scotland, without individual parish descriptions. 'But I found such merit and ability, and so many useful facts and important observations in the answers that were sent to me,' he wrote, 'that I could not think of depriving the clergy of the credit.'

The statistical accounts should not be confused with financial accounts. These are descriptions of the landscape, the crops, and the fish in the rivers and the sea, but they also cover the price of food and clothing, the number

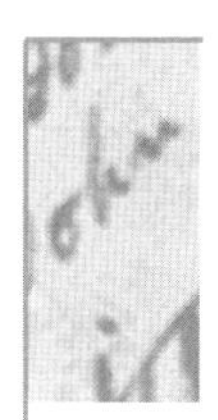

of people who lived in the parish, how superstitious they were and whether they spoke Gaelic or broad Scots.

The first Statistical Account was so well received that a New Statistical Account was published between 1834 and 1845, containing contributions from local doctors, teachers and landowners. The first volume of a Third Statistical Account was published in 1951, but the final volumes didn't appear until 1992. For East Lothian (whose Third Account was published in 1953), a Fourth Statistical Account was published between 2003 and 2009.

People and their dress

It would be excellent if you could find your ancestors mentioned by name, but unfortunately, relatively few individuals are named in the accounts. It is still worth trying to find your ancestors, however, as you may just be lucky.

If your ancestor owned land, then you probably will be able to find him or her, as the major land-owners in the parish (the 'heritors') are usually named in the accounts. In the 1843 account of Tibbermore in Perthshire, we learn that the parish had previously consisted of two baronies, one of which, Huntingtower, had been divided up and sold by the Duke of Atholl about 30 years before.

'These properties were chiefly purchased by men who made their own fortunes, and were the founders of their own families,' writes account's author. 'Those heritors who possess land in the parish of the yearly value of £50 and upwards' included General Cunningham of Newton and Huntingtower; Thomas Ritchie of the Hill of Ruthven and South Black Ruthven; William Dron of North Black Ruthven and Marlefield; the Revd. Dr. Thomson of Ruthven Farm; William S. Turnbull of Ruthven Mills; Thomas Duncan of Ruthven Field ; Mrs. Black of Law Grove; John Martin of Newhouse; Thomas Millar of Letham; James Macmillan of Alexandria; and D. S. McLagan of Ruthven House.

The 1835 account of the town of Elgin in Moray mentions Lieutenant-General Andrew Anderson, late of the East India Company. We are told that General Anderson was born of very humble parents in the neighbouring parish of Lhanbryd, and entered the Company's service as a private soldier.

> 'By his good conduct and soldierly qualities he attained rank and wealth,' says the account, 'and the large fortune which he had honourably acquired he devoted at his death to the education of the young, and the support of the aged poor of his native county. The Elgin

Institution [built in 1832 and now a care home] at the east end of the town is a splendid memorial of this philanthropist.'

Perhaps an ancestor or relative of yours is one of the 'eminent men' born in Langholm, Dumfriesshire, who are mentioned in its new account, also compiled in 1835. The men include 'Mr. [John] Maxwell, the ingenious author of *An Essay upon Tune*; John Pasley, an enterprising and successful London merchant; Admiral Sir Thomas Pasley, his brother, who distinguished himself under Earl Howe, in the defeat of the French fleet, on the 1st of June 1794; William Julius Meikle, the translator of [Portuguese author] Camoens' *Lusiad*; and Colonels Matthew Murray and John Little, who distinguished themselves under the Marquis Cornwallis, in the wars against Tippoo Saib [ruler of Mysore in south India].'

In addition, there are 'Captain George Maxwell, R.N. who signalized himself [i.e. made himself remarkable] in an engagement with the Dutch, off the Dogger Bank in 1781; Ralph Irvine M.D., who died in India, 1795, a young man of great promise in his profession; Colonel C. Pasley of the Royal Engineers, well known for his attainments in literature and science, who has now withdrawn from the active duties of life, and is enjoying his well-earned fame among the scenes of his infancy; and David Irvine LL.D. author of the *Life of George Buchanan*, etc. and librarian to the Faculty of Advocates.'

In his detailed account of Cambuslang in Lanarkshire in 1791, the Revd. Dr. James Meek compares the clothing worn 40 years previously with that worn in 1790. He writes that in 1750, 'when a farmer's family went to the kirk, or to a market, he and his sons wore suits of home-made cloth, plaiden hose, and blue or black bonnets; his wife and daughters were dressed in gowns of their own spinning, cloth cloaks and hoods, worsted stockings and leather shoes.'

Dr. Meek adds that by 1790, in contrast, the men 'wore suits of English cloth, worsted or cotton stockings and hats', while the women 'were dressed in printed callico or silk gowns, scarlet or silk cloaks, silk bonnets, white thread stockings, and cloth shoes.'

Ghosts, fairies and witches

In the 1790s account of Clunie, Perthshire, the Revd. William McRitchie states that:

'superstitions, charms and incantations have lost their power. Cats, hares, magpies and old women cease to assume any other appearance than what nature has given them; and ghosts, goblins, witches and fairies have relinquished the land.'

At the same time, however, the Revd. John Grant insists that such beliefs are still alive and well in the parish of Kirkmichael, Banffshire.

> 'On the sequestered hill, and in the darksome valley,' writes the Revd. Grant, 'frequently does the benighted traveller behold the visionary semblance of his departed friend, perhaps of his enemy. These illusions of fancy operate sometimes with such force, that several have died in consequence of them; and some have been deprived of their reason.'

Also firmly established in the area was a belief in fairies, who lived in 'detached hillocks covered with verdure, situated on the banks of purling brooks, or surrounded by thickets of wood.'

The Revd. Grant describes how: 'In the autumnal season, when the moon shines from a serene sky, often is the wayfaring traveller arrested by the music of the hills. Often struck with a more solemn scene, he beholds the visionary hunters engaged in the chase, and pursuing the deer of the clouds, while the hollow rocks in long-sounding echoes reverberate their cries.'

He adds that 'there are several now living, who assert that they have seen and heard this aerial hunting, and that they have been suddenly surrounded by visionary forms, and assailed by a multitude of voices, louder than the noise of rushing waters.'

Then the Revd. Grant tells a curious story about a clergyman in Banffshire around 50 years earlier. 'One night as he was returning home, at a late hour, he was seized by the fairies, and carried aloft into the air,' he relates. 'Through fields of ether and fleecy clouds he journeyed many a mile, descrying the earth far distant below him, and no bigger than a nut-shell. Being thus sufficiently convinced of the reality of their existence, they let him down at the door of his own house, where he afterward often recited to the wondering circle, the marvelous tale of his adventure.'

If anyone claimed that this had happened to him today, it would be put into the category of alleged abductions by aliens, rather than fairies! We might also wonder (maybe quite unfairly) whether, instead of coming from a church meeting, as the Revd. Grant states, the earlier clergyman was perhaps returning home from an inn!

As well as ghosts and fairies, Kirkmichael people also believed in witchcraft and magic.

> 'Even at present, witches are supposed, as of old, to ride on broom-sticks through the air,' says the Revd. Grant. 'In this country, the 12th of May is one of their festivals. On the morning of that day, they are frequently seen dancing on the surface of the water of Avon,

brushing the dews of the lawn, and milking cows in their fold. Any uncommon sickness is generally attributed to their demoniacal practices. They make fields barren or fertile, raise or still whirlwinds, give or take away milk at pleasure.'

In an area where the people had such beliefs, there was always someone who would take advantage of them, an 'anti-conjurer' as the Revd. Grant names him.

'If the spouse is jealous of her husband, the anti-conjurer is consulted to restore the affections of his bewitched heart,' he writes. 'If a near connection lies confined to the bed of sickness, it is in vain to expect relief without the balsamic medicine of the anti-conjurer. If a person happens to be deprived of his senses, the deranged cells of the brain must be adjusted by the magic charms of the anti-conjurer. If a farmer loses his cattle, the houses must be purified with water sprinkled by him.'

Books and websites

In her book *Parish Life in Eighteenth-Century Scotland: A Review of the Old Statistical Account*, nutritionist Maisie Steven points out that when we read the accounts, we are being exposed to the viewpoints and prejudices of their authors. For example, the Revd. Alexander MacPherson, minister of Golspie, Sutherland, writing shortly after the infamous Highland Clearances never once mentions the evictions that took place in the parish.

MacPherson describes (like the sycophantic clergyman Mr. Collins in Jane Austen's *Pride and Prejudice*) the exemplary character of his patrons the Duke and Duchess of Sutherland, however, and writes 'nor is it too much to say that the system of farming at present followed in this parish does not fall short of the best modes of farming in any part of the kingdom'.

All of the Old and New Statistical Accounts are available online, free of charge, at **http://edina.ac.uk/stat-acc-scot**. You can also take out a subscription, which provides enhanced searching, cut-and-paste facilities and some other resources. These include Sir John Sinclair's analysis of the Old Accounts in 1826, maps of the counties showing the parishes (mostly in colour), the manuscript accounts of the parishes of Dumfries, Forgandenny (Perthshire) and Stow (Midlothian) and the 1801 census of Stow (a rare survival).

Some of the Old and New published accounts have been digitised and are available online at the Internet Archive **www.archive.org** (and some also at Google Books **http://books.google.co.uk**). Published volumes of the Third Statistical Account can be ordered from online booksellers such as Amazon **www.amazon.co.uk**, as can print-on-demand copies of the volumes of the two earlier sets of accounts. You can find out more about the Fourth Statistical Account of East Lothian at **www.el4.org.uk/wb**.

Statistical accounts elsewhere

Sir John Sinclair's publications inspired a similar Statistical Account of Ireland, but only three volumes were published from 1814-1819. Most of the north of Ireland was covered by the Ordnance Survey Memoirs compiled in the 1830s, but all but one parish account remained unpublished until 1993.

Unfortunately, Sir John was unsuccessful in drumming up interest for a Statistical Account of England, although a few parish accounts were published locally (such as those of Preston, Lancsahire and St. Just in Penwith, Cornwall, published in 1821 and 1842 respectively). You can find the Statistical Accounts of Ireland, Preston and St. Just at the Internet Archive and Google Books, as well as similarly titled books on the Isle of Man and parts of Canada, Australia, India and the USA.

In the library of the Society of Genealogists

The Society's library has a complete set of printed volumes of the 'Old' Statistical Account of the 1790s, and some volumes of the New Statistical Account of the 1830s/1840s.

CHAPTER THIRTEEN
Services of Heirs

As mentioned in Chapter 7 (Wills and Inventories), under Scots Law, land and buildings were 'heritable' as opposed to 'moveable' property. While moveable property could be bequeathed by means of a testament testamentar, until the passage of the Heritable Jurisdictions Act in 1868, heritable property was passed on through the law of inheritance.

Usually, the eldest surviving son succeeded his father, but if there were no sons, the property would be divided in equal portions between the daughters, who were known as 'heirs portioner'. (This has nothing to do with male portioners, who were simply owners of a portion of land.)

If the deceased person had no children, then the next *younger* brother would succeed to the property (as 'heir of line') if it had been inherited, while the next *older* brother would succeed (as 'heir of conquest') if the deceased had purchased the property.

Up to 1847, the person or persons wishing to inherit the property would, in many cases, be 'served heir to' the deceased through a 'retour' (return) containing the verdict of a jury assembled by a judge or judges to investigate the claim. The jury, composed of people (often family members

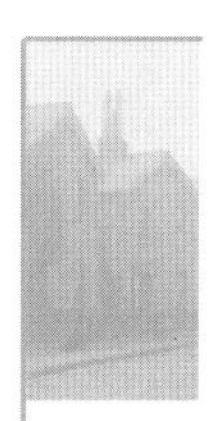

or friends) who would know whether the claim was justified, issued a retour (in Latin). 'Special' retours name the land in question, while 'general' retours don't.

After 1847, a claimant would issue a 'petition of service' to a local court or the Sheriff in Chancery, and if successful, a 'decree of service' would be issued by the sheriff of the county or the Sheriff in Chancery.

In 1863, the first of four volumes was published containing 10-year indexes to the services of heirs from 1 January 1700 to 31 December 1859. The indexes contain a short description ('distinguishing particulars') of each service (in English) including the date of service (and very occasionally the date of death) and the date of recording, which may be several (and sometimes very many) years later.

While the main indexes are alphabetical by the surname of the person served (i.e. the heir), there are also supplementary indexes, which are alphabetical by the surname of the person being served to (i.e. the deceased), where the two surnames are different. This is helpful, as it may then lead you to the will of a family member you were unaware of.

Some examples from the main indexes are:

> Grahame - Hugh, [served heir] to his father George Grahame, writer in Fortrose, who died 2nd January 1718 - Heir Male Special in houses and portions of ground in the burgh of Fortrose, Ross-shire - 17 February 1719. [Date of recording] 1720, Nov. 28.

> Ralston - Janet - (or *Patrick*), Widow of Wm. Ralston, Cushnocksteps, [served heir] to her brother James Patrick, merchant, Glasgow - Heir Portioner General - 23 October 1775. [Date of recording] 1775, Nov. 7.

> Murdoch - John, shoemaker, Stirling, [served heir] to his brother Patrick Murdoch, candlemaker there - Heir General - 13 June 1788. [Date of recording] 1814, Nov. 1.

Unfortunately, there's no overall index to the services of heirs, but all four volumes of the 10-year indexes have been digitised and are available on CD from the Scottish Genealogy Society (see Chapter 17). The society has also issued a CD containing indexed summaries (in Latin, apart from the years 1652-1659) of retours from 1545-1699.

In the library of the Society of Genealogists

You can view both CDs using one of the computers in the Society's Lower Library.

CHAPTER FOURTEEN
Scottish Legal Records

Land records

In Scotland, most land had been held through the feudal system until 28 November 2004, when the Abolition of Feudal Tenure (Scotland) Act 2000 came into force. All land had been held in a hierarchical structure under the Crown, with the people at the bottom of the pyramid known as 'vassals', while those above them were their 'feudal superiors' to whom 'feu duty' had to be paid (in lieu of the military service originally required). That system has been replaced by one in which land is owned outright by the former vassals and there are neither feudal superiors nor feu duty.

When a vassal died, his heir could prove his right to inherit by obtaining a 'retour' or 'service of heir' (see Chapter 13). Whether land or buildings had been inherited or purchased, the transaction had to be recorded in the appropriate 'sasine' (pronounced '*say*-zin') register, which recorded the transfer of ownership.

However, you have to bear in mind, as the National Records of Scotland (NRS) warns in its online guide to sasines **www.nas.gov.uk/guides/sasines.asp**, that most Scots people were tenants rather than land-owners before the 20th century, and so will be found in neither the registers of sasines nor the retours of services of heirs.

The earliest (and incomplete) register, known as the 'Secretary's Register' (SR), was kept from 1599-1609, and then from 1617, 'particular registers' (PRs) of sasines were kept for most counties, as was a 'general registers of sasines' covering all of Scotland except the three Lothian counties. These registers were replaced in 1869 by one general register in county divisions. In addition, Scotland's 66 'royal burghs' kept their own sasine registers.

According to the NRS (which holds all the registers except Glasgow's and those of Aberdeen and Dundee before 1809), the sasine registers are 'fairly complete' from 1617 and 'fully comprehensive' from about 1660, although in the case of an eldest son inheriting a property, he might not have had a sasine executed until much later.

Beginning in 1821 (and going back to 1781), short summaries or 'abridgements' of the sasine records were compiled (but not for burgh records). Here is an example of the abridgement of a conveyance in the Particular Register of Sasines for Aberdeenshire:

> **Date:** Dec. 2. 1852
>
> RODERICK GRAY residing in Peterhead, *Seised*, - in a piece of unimproved ground containing 2 roods and 20 poles on the Middlemuirs commonly called the Clayholes, in the burgh of INVERURY, parish of Inverury; - on Feu Charter by the magistrates of Inverury, with consent of the trustees of William Lundie residing in Inverury, and the said William Lundie, Oct. 2. 1852. P.R. 249. 148.

The original conveyancing document (a charter) is in volume 249 of the Particular Register, beginning at folio 148.

Since 1981, the registers of sasines are gradually being replaced by a Land Register. The NRS has an electronic index to the sasines from 1781 onwards, and all the sasines are in the process of being digitised. You can view the index and the sasines that have been digitised at the NRS in Edinburgh, but they are not yet available online.

The website of the Friends of Dundee City Archives **www.fdca.org.uk** has an index of the 1831-32 Dundee sasines (under 'Burgh Records').

Sasine indexes in the library of the Society of Genealogists

The Society of Genealogists holds (mostly printed) indexes to the:

- General Register of Sasines (1701-1720);
- SR and PR of Sasines for Aberdeenshire (1599-1609 and 1617-1660);
- PR of Sasines for Argyll, Bute, and Dumbartonshire (1617-1780);
- SR and PR of Sasines for Ayrshire (1599-1609 and 1617-1660);
- SR and PR of Sasines for Banffshire (1600-1609 and 1617-1780);
- PR of Sasines for Berwickshire (1617-1780);
- PR of Sasines for Caithness (1646-1780) - before 1646 part of Inverness-shire;
- PR of Sasines for Dumfriesshire and Kirkcudbrightshire (1617-1780);
- SR and PR of Sasines for the Lothians (1599-1609 and 1617-1660);
- PR of Sasines for Elginshire (Moray) and Nairnshire (1617-1780);
- SR and PR of Sasines for Fife and Kinross-shire (1603-1609 and 1617-1660);
- PR of Sasines for Forfarshire (Angus) (1620-1700);
- PR of Sasines for Forfarshire (Angus) (1701-1780) - on microfiche;
- PR of Sasines for Inverness-shire, Ross & Cromarty and Sutherland (1661-1780);
- SR and PR of Sasines for Kincardineshire (1600-1608 and 1617-1657);
- PR of Sasines for Lanarkshire (1618-1780);
- PR of Sasines for Orkney and Shetland (1617-1660) - on microfiche.

Criminal court records

The NAS has an online guide to crime and criminals **www.nas.gov.uk/guides/crime.asp** that describes the various Scottish courts, which are quite different to those of England and Wales. The NAS catalogue **www.nas.gov.uk/onlineCatalogue** contains brief information on criminal trials.

Here is an example of what you may find:

Reference: JC26/1829/62

Title: Trial papers relating to Donald Henderson, Robert Sutherland, John Bruce for the crime of mobbing and rioting at Dunbeath, Latheron, Caithness. Tried at High Court, Inverness.

Date: 27 April 1829

Accused: Donald Henderson, son of Robert Henderson, senior. Verdict: outlawed. Sentence: sentence of fugitation.
Robert Sutherland. Verdict: guilty. Sentence: transportation - 7 years.
John Bruce, son of Helen Gunn or Bruce. Verdict: outlawed. Sentence: sentence of fugitation.

Victim: John Gunn, Dunbeath, Latheron, Caithness.
John Wallace, Borgue, Langwell or Berriedale Estate, Latheron, Caithness.
George Bain, Bienacheilt, Latheron.

The crime of 'mobbing and rioting' meant forming part of a mob engaged in disorderly criminal behavior, in this case, probably protesting against the infamous Highland Clearances. The two men who were outlawed appear not to have been in court, while a sentence of 'fugitation' meant that their goods and chattels were seized by the court.

Court records in the library of the Society of Genealogists

The SoG library holds some published transcripts of the records of various Scottish law courts, including those of:

- The High Court of Justiciary in Edinburgh 1661-1678;
- The sheriff courts of Aberdeenshire from before 1600 to 1680, Fife 1515-1522, Orkney and Shetland 1614-1615, and Shetland 1602-1604;
- The burgh courts of Kinkintilloch (Dunbartonshire) 1658-1694, Lochmaben (Dumfriesshire) 1612-1721, and Selkirk 1503-1545.

The library also holds transcripts of the records of several 'franchise' courts, where up to 1747, justice was administered by local land-owners (something like the manorial courts of England and Wales):

- The baron courts of Carnwath (Lanarkshire) 1523-1542, Corshill (Ayrshire) 1666-1719, Forbes (Aberdeenshire) 1659-1678, Skene, Leys and Whitehaugh (Aberdeenshire and Kincardineshire) 1613-1687, Stitchill (Roxburghshire) 1655-1807, and Urie (Kincardineshire) 1604-1747.
- The regality courts of Melrose (Roxburghshire) 1605-1609 and 1657-1661, and Spynie (Moray) 1592-1601.

CHAPTER FIFTEEN

More Online Sources for Scottish Family History

Apart from ScotlandsPeople **www.scotlandspeople.gov.uk**, already mentioned in connection with the Scottish civil registration records, census returns, parish registers, Roman Catholic registers, wills and inventories, and coats of arms, there are many other websites with information on Scottish people.

Ancestry.co.uk (payment site)

As well as the records already covered in previous chapters, the subscription site Ancestry.co.uk **www.ancestry.co.uk** has several other Scottish databases, including:

- Index cards for libraries in Cupar (Fife) from 1833-1987 and Perth 1809-1990;
- Fife voters' lists 1832-1894;
- Fife & Kinross Register 1814;
- Fife, Kinross& Clackmannan Register 1903, 1905, 1908, 1912, 1914 and 1917;
- The *Dunfermline Register* 1829-1859;
- Perthshire school registers 1869-1902;
- Perthshire cess, stent and valuation rolls 1650-1899;

- Perth militia survey 1802, Register of Deeds 1566-1811 and surveys of inhabitants (heads of household censuses) 1766 and 1773;
- Gretna Green marriage registers 1794-1895;
- *Fasti Ecclesiae Scoticanae* (details of more than 2,000 ministers of the Church of Scotland);
- Edinburgh Almanac 1853;
- *Historic Families of Scotland*;
- Gazetteers of Scotland;
- Some extracted parish records for more than 20 of the historic counties.

Scottish Strays Marriage Index (free)

The Anglo-Scottish Family History Society, a specialist branch of the Manchester & Lancashire Family History Society, has compiled a Scottish Strays Marriage Index at **www.anglo-scots.mlfhs.org.uk**. The index mainly lists marriages that took place outside Scotland, and where at least one spouse was born in Scotland. A reference number is usually given, so you can make contact via the society with the person who supplied the information.

FamilySearch (free)

The International Genealogical Index (IGI) on the LDS FamilySearch website **www.familysearch.org** is particularly useful for Scottish research, as almost all baptisms and marriages/banns listed in the OPRs are indexed in the IGI or in one of the two Scottish databases (for baptisms and marriages respectively) at the newer version of the FamilySearch site **https://www.familysearch.org**.

The IGI also holds births and marriages from the Scottish statutory records for the period 1855-1875. In addition, you can carry out a search for all the children of a couple by specifying the forenames and surnames of the parents.

(The Family Search website also allows you to search the 1881 census of England, Wales, the Isle of Man, and the Channel Islands. The Scottish 1881 census, however, is available as digital images only from ScotlandsPeople and as a transcription from Ancestry.co.uk and Findmypast.)

Deceased Online (payment site)

This pay-per-view website (with free searching), which aims to be the central database for UK burials and cremations, includes transcriptions of many Scottish cremation and burial records. At the time of writing (March 2012), these covered:

- Aberdeen (192,000 burials in 10 cemeteries/churchyards);
- Aberdeenshire (33,828 burials in Peterhead cemetery and churchyard);
- Angus (190,000 burials in over 75 cemeteries/churchyards);
- Edinburgh (224,620 cremations at Warriston Crematorium, 49,502 cremations at Seafield Crematorium and 38,629 burials in Seafield Cemetery);
- Scottish Monumental Inscriptions (90,000 headstone images from 165 cemeteries/churchyards, including 10,877 in Angus; 2,160 in Clackmannanshire; 912 in Edinburgh; 39,732 in Fife; 4,500 in the Highland area; 15,222 in Lanarkshire; 6,020 in Perthshire; and 8,266 in West Lothian).

Other useful Scottish websites (free unless stated otherwise)

- Ask Scotland **http://askscotland.org.uk** lets you ask a question online, which will be answered by a librarian;
- Ayrshire Ancestors **www.ayrshireancestors.com** - pay-per-view database of monumental inscriptions and birth, marriage and death extracts from the *Ayr Advertiser* newspaper;
- Ayrshire Roots **www.ayrshireroots.com** holds several databases relating to the county;
- Badbea Families **www.badbeafamilies.com** has information about the families moved to Badbea, Caithness during the Highland Clearances;
- Burke's Peerage and Gentry **www.burkespeerage.com** - a subscription database of 15,000 British and Irish family records from the printed volumes of *Burke's Peerage, Baronetage and Knightage* (titled people) and *Burke's Landed Gentry* (untitled people). The site contains a library of free articles (including many on Scottish social history, royal lineage and historic families), as well as links to Scottish family history websites and other sites;
- County Sutherland **www.countysutherland.co.uk** - many population lists and other information for the 13 parishes in the county of Sutherland;
- Friends of Dundee City Archives **www.fdca.org.uk** has databases of the city's burgess roll from 1513 to the present, the 1801 census, 1865/66 voters' roll, list of 19th century ships, poorhouse records, directories, Methodist baptisms 1785-1898, burials and mortcloth hire records from the 16th-19th centuries, records of Cowgate School, war memorials, and vehicle registrations, as well as research guides;
- Friends of Perth & Kinross Council Archive **www.pkc.gov.uk** (go to 'Archives' and then 'Friends of the Archive') includes databases of Perth Burgh burial registers 1794-1855 (and beyond), 17th-19th century Perthshire militia records, First and Second World War sources, and women's sources in the archive;
- Gazetteer for Scotland **www.scottish-places.info** includes a transcription of the 19th century *Ordnance Gazetteer of Scotland*;

- Glasgow Southern Necropolis **www.southernnecropolis.com** - includes an alphabetical list of some of the burials;
- Graven Images **http://graven-images.org.uk** has photographs and transcriptions of some Caithness graveyards, as well as two digitised books on the county's leading families and its ministers;
- Highland Archives **www.internet-promotions.co.uk/archives** - all about Caithness, particularly military matters;
- Mull Genealogy **www.mullgenealogy.co.uk** - includes birth and (worldwide) burial indexes, and a search of 1841-1901 censuses and other population listings;
- North Perthshire Family History Group **www.npfhg.org/resources.htm** - with some census, death and burial transcriptions;
- Orkney Genealogy **www.cursiter.com** - contains baptisms and marriages from the International Genealogical Index (IGI) for many surnames for Orkney, and also for Caithness and Shetland;
- Roots Hebrides **www.rootshebrides.com** - information on tracing your ancestry in the Western Isles, with many contact details (including the *Co Leis Thu?* genealogy centre, which has 30,000 detailed family trees, and local historical societies) and several case studies;
- Ross & Cromarty Roots **www.rosscromartyroots.co.uk** - includes transcriptions and photographs of monumental inscriptions in 36 burial grounds;
- Scots at War Trust **www.scotsatwar.org.uk** - includes a roll of honour, and links to other rolls;
- Scottish emigration database **www.abdn.ac.uk/emigration** - contains the records of over 21,000 emigrants;
- Scottish National War Memorial **www.snwm.org** - includes a search of the entries in the memorial in Edinburgh Castle;
- Talking Scot **www.talkingscot.com** - family history discussion forum;
- Tour Scotland **www.fife.50megs.com** has photographs of more than 30 Scottish churchyards;
- Virtual Mitchell **www.mitchelllibrary.org/virtualmitchell** - old photographs of Glasgow.

Portals to yet more Scottish websites (the portals are all free)

- GENUKI **www.genuki.org.uk/big/sct**;
- Scotland GenWeb **www.scotlandgenweb.org**;
- Census Finder **www.censusfinder.com/scotland.htm**;
- Cyndi's List **www.cyndislist.com/uk/sct**;
- UKBMD **www.ukbmd.co.uk**;
- UKGDL **www.ukgdl.org.uk**;
- UKMFH **www.ukmfh.org.uk;**

- UKIsearch **www.ukisearch.com/scotland.html**;
- Scotland's Family **www.scotlandsfamily.com**.

Future Scottish online records

The records of kirk sessions (local church courts dealing with moral transgressions among other things) of both the Church of Scotland parishes and some of the secession churches have been made available online. The digital images can be viewed at the NRS in Edinburgh and in a number of Scottish local archives. The records had been expected to be made available online in late 2011, but at the time of writing (March 2012), this had not yet happened.

In addition, the NRS intends to put High Court of Justiciary records online, and is also digitising 19th century poor relief registers (beginning with those of the historic counties of Caithness, Ross & Cromarty, and Wigtownshire). Other records that may be made available online in the future include 'sasines' (land records), fatal accident inquiries and taxation records, although these are all longer-term projects.

100 Years Celebration
SOCIETY OF GENEALOGISTS

CHAPTER SIXTEEN

Scottish Resources in the SoG Library

The Library of the Society of Genealogists holds many resources for Scottish family history, including transcriptions and indexes in microform and book format. In addition, the Society provides Internet access at no charge to several commercial websites and, of course, to all the free sites mentioned in this book.

Although some of the books in the Society's library are available online in digitised form, not everyone has Internet access at home, and many of us prefer to use a printed copy of a book if we can.

You can find a review of Scottish resources in the library on the SoG website at **www.sog.org.uk/prc/sct.shtml**, which gives a general review of resources for the whole of Scotland, as well as for the 33 historic counties. The page lists the parishes and other places on which the Society has material.

For detailed information on SoG holdings, you need to search the Society's online catalogue SOGCAT at **http://62.32.98.6/S10312UKStaff/OPAC**.

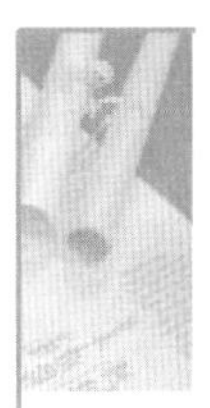

Middle Library

Material on the Scottish (SC) shelves in the Society's Middle Library is grouped in the following categories:

SC/G	General
SC/L	Local
SC/R	Registers
SC/M	Monumental inscriptions
SC/C	Censuses
SC/D	Directories
SC/P	Poll Books
SC/PER	Periodicals

The 'general' category includes sources that cover the whole of Scotland and these can include diverse subjects such as apprentices, army, courts and criminals, emigrants, maps and topography, militia and musters, newspapers, taxation, and wills.

In its 'periodical' category, the library holds 140 volumes of record transcriptions published by the Scottish Record Society (SRS). Nearly 30 of these volumes are indexes of testaments confirmed by the old commissary courts. There are also 36 volumes of 17th and 18th century indexes to the Registers of Sasines (land transfer records), and 46 volumes of indexes to the Register of Deeds from 1661-1714.

For Edinburgh, there are a number of SRS volumes of burial and MI transcriptions, registers of apprentices covering the period 1583-1800, and rolls of burgesses and guild brethren from 1406-1841.

The SoG holds the *Fasti Ecclesiae Scoticanae* in seven volumes, which gives brief information on all the Church of Scotland (CoS) ministers since the Reformation. There are also several books on the history of the CoS, the Free Church and the other secession churches.

You'll also find the 'Old' Statistical Account of Scotland (published between 1791 and 1799), as well as some volumes of the New Statistical Account (published in the 1830s and 1840s). The library has books on the clans, families and surnames of Scotland and on tracing Scottish ancestry, as well as holding the journals of the various Scottish family history societies.

The SoG has 54 volumes of court records, 45 volumes of poll books and lists of electors (including burgess rolls and lists of freeholders) and 11 volumes of *Extracts from Glasgow Burgh Records*.

You can find transcriptions of the 1691 Hearth Tax assessments for Angus, Ayrshire, East Lothian, Perthshire, Renfrewshire (also on CD, together with the 1696 Poll Tax schedules) and West Lothian. There are also Valuations of Aberdeenshire and Wigtownshire in 1667, 1694-1696 Poll Tax lists for Aberdeenshire, Edinburgh and Paisley and population lists for Assynt, Sutherland from 1638-1811.

The library holds 21 volumes of the *Proceedings of the Society of Antiquaries of Scotland*, many volumes of the Scottish Historical Review, various reports of the Historical Manuscripts Commission, and many volumes of the publications of the Scottish History Society, the Spalding Club (of Aberdeen) and the Stair Society (concerned with the history of Scots Law).

Upper Library

In the SoG's Upper Library, you'll find registers/histories of Aberdeen, Edinburgh, Glasgow and St. Andrews Universities, as well as those of at least 16 Scottish schools. Also on the upper floor are regimental histories, histories of families, one-name studies and peerage/landed gentry directories.

Lower Library

On the Society's web page **www.sog.org.uk/library/surnames_and_families.shtml**, you'll find surname indexes to the Surname Document Collection, pedigrees and birth briefs. The Surname Document Collection consists of original documents and transcriptions, such as civil registration birth, marriage and death certificates, parish register entries, wills, deeds, family trees and research notes.

Among the Society's Special Collections, the MacLeod Papers are of particular interest for Scottish research, covering more than 600 family names. These papers consist of the notes of the Revd. Walter MacLeod and his son John, who were professional genealogists in Edinburgh. The MacLeod Papers are included in the card index to the Special Collections, which you'll find in the Society's Lower Library.

The SoG has a very large collection of pedigrees (family trees), most of which are in the form of roll pedigrees. The Society's birth brief collection contains around

28,000 surnames taken from members' birth brief forms, which show a member's ancestry back four generations to his or her great-great-grandparents.

The Lower Library is where you'll find the Society's computers, with free Internet access to Ancestry.co.uk (which has transcriptions of the Scottish censuses from 1841-1901), Findmypast, the Origins Network, Family Relatives and The National Archives' Documents Online.

The Society also has various CDs (such as those published by the Scottish Genealogy Society indexing the Services of Heirs), microfiche and microfilms (including the Scottish civil registration indexes from 1855-1920, images of the actual records for 1855, which contain more information than in later years, many parish register copies and some census returns - particularly for 1851 - as well as indexes to wills, sasines and deeds).

CHAPTER SEVENTEEN

Scottish Archives and Family History Societies

National Records of Scotland

In April 2011, the General Register Office for Scotland (GROS) and the National Archives of Scotland (NAS) merged under the name National Records of Scotland. At the time of writing (March 2012), however, the two organisations still had separate websites, although a portal site had been set up at **www.nrscotland.gov.uk**.

At the GROS site **www.gro-scotland.gov.uk**, you'll find helpful online leaflets and a list of parish registers showing the years covered for baptisms, marriages and burials. The NAS site **www.nas.gov.uk** has many useful online guides to its records, and an online public access catalogue (OPAC), in which you can search for soldiers' and airmen's wills (among other records).

Even before their amalgamation, the GROS and NAS were working as partners (together with the heraldic Court of the Lord Lyon) in the ScotlandsPeople website **www.scotlandspeople.gov.uk** and the ScotlandsPeople Centre **www.scotlandspeoplehub.gov.uk** in Edinburgh, which physically unites General Register House and New Register House, the homes of the NAS and GROS respectively.

National Library of Scotland

The National Library of Scotland (NLS) **www.nls.uk** is Scotland's main reference library. The NLS website holds Scottish directories from 1773-1911 (see Chapter 3), maps of Scotland (see Chapter 10) and a catalogue that you can search online.

Scottish Archive Network

The website of the Scottish Archive Network (SCAN) **www.scan.org.uk** contains an online catalogue for 52 Scottish local archives, and its Digital Archive includes the Highlands and Islands Emigration Society database of 5,000 emigrants to Australia between 1852 and 1857, and the Lieutenancy Book for the County of Roxburgh 1797-1802 (militia lists for all the Roxburghshire parishes).

Scottish Association of Family History Societies

The Scottish Association of Family History Societies (SAFHS) is an 'umbrella organisation', whose members include 27 family history societies in Scotland and eight overseas societies with Scottish interest groups. At the association's website **www.safhs.org.uk**, you'll find links to most of those societies, a list of the association's publications, and downloadable copies of the six-monthly SAFHS Bulletins, which include news from the member societies.

Scottish family history societies

At the website of the Scottish Genealogy Society (SGS) **www.scotsgenealogy.com**, you can view 'The Black Book', a listing that includes the society's holdings of monumental inscription (MI) lists for each parish in a county. Many of these MI lists can be bought from the society's online shop. The SGS site also has a cumulative index of the society's journal from 1953-2005, an index of members' family history research, and links to local archives, some online digitised books and much more.

The Aberdeen & North East Scotland FHS **www.anesfhs.org.uk** has online searchable databases including an index of its MI booklets; the Aberdeen 'Stent Roll' (an assessment for tax) for 1669; burials at St. Nicholas' Church, Aberdeen from 1666-1793; baptisms at St. Paul's Episcopal Church, Aberdeen from 1720-1793; and St. Nicholas Kirk Session Accounts from 1602-1705.

You can search indexes of MIs, magazine articles, Poor Law records and members' family trees at the Borders FHS website **www.bordersfhs.org.uk**. The site also has parish maps for the four Scottish Borders counties, as well as a great deal of helpful information for family history research in each parish.

The Fife FHS has many record transcriptions online at **http://fifefhs.org/Records/recordsindex.htm**, either related to the whole county or to a specific parish. The site also has a number of photographs on its site.

The Highland FHS's resource page at **www.highlandfamilyhistorysociety.org/HFHSResource.htm** includes indexes of article topics, MI transcriptions, 'strays' (Highlanders recorded away from their home parishes) and queries published in the society's journal.

The Moray Burial Ground Research Group's website **www.mbgrg.org** has a searchable index of MIs in the present-day Moray unitary authority, which includes part of the historic county of Banffshire.

At the Moray & Nairn FHS site **www.morayandnairnfhs.co.uk**, you can find transcriptions of Moray and Nairnshire 'miscellanies' and archived copies of the society's newsletter (including a *Brief History of Moray and Nairn*).

The North Perthshire Family History Group **www.npfhg.org** has downloadable transcriptions of Logierait burials from 1764-1815, Fortingall deaths from 1855-1938, and the censuses of Fortingall in 1881 and Kirkmichael in 1851, 1891 and 1901.

As a member of the Orkney FHS **www.orkneyfhs.co.uk**, you can view all the Orkney censuses, MIs, information on parishes, Poor Law lists, past issues of the society's *Sib Folk News* magazine and society members' family trees.

The website of the West Lothian FHS **www.wlfhs.org.uk** contains photographs and transcriptions of the names on the county's war memorials, and old photographs of its towns and villages.

In the library of the Society of Genealogists

The Society's library contains many issues of the journals/magazines published by the Scottish family history societies.

Many of these books are no longer in publication, but you can usually buy copies from a second-hand bookshop or online through Amazon **www.amazon.co.uk** or Abebooks **www.abebooks.co.uk**. In addition, you can find many out-of-copyright Scottish books at the Internet Archive **www.archive.org** or at Google Books **http://books.google.co.uk**.

Tracing Scottish Ancestry

In Search of Scottish Ancestry, Gerald Hamilton Edwards.

Tracing Your Scottish Ancestry, Kathleen B. Cory.

Gathering the Clans: Tracing Scottish Ancestry on the Internet, Alan Stewart.

Tracing Your Scottish Ancestors: the Official Guide, National Records of Scotland (first edition by Cecil Sinclair) - a detailed guide to the records held by the NRS.

Sources for Scottish Genealogy and Family History, D.J. Steel (part XII of the SoG's *National Index of Parish Registers*) - good on nonconformist and secession churches.

Scottish Ancestry, Sherry Irvine - a North American book, good on research from a distance and using the LDS Family History Library and Centres. Has a 22-page bibliography.

Discover Your Scottish Ancestry, Graham S. Holton and Jack Winch. Also has a 22-page bibliography.

Researching Scottish Family History, Chris Paton - good on occupations.

The Scottish Family Tree Detective, Rosemary Bigwood - good on occupations and legal documents, and includes a list of parishes with their historic county, current unitary authority, sheriff court and commissary court.

Scottish Genealogy, Bruce Durie - good on old handwriting and DNA testing.

Records and their whereabouts

The Hearth Tax, Other Later Stuart Tax Lists and the Association Oath Rolls, Jeremy Gibson (also covers the Poll Tax).

Land and Window Tax Assessments, Jeremy Gibson, Mervyn Medlycott and Dennis Mills (also mentions other taxes).

Tudor and Stuart Muster Rolls, Jeremy Gibson and Alan Dell.
Militia Lists and Musters 1757-1876, Jeremy Gibson and Mervyn Medlycott.
Registers of the Secession Churches in Scotland, Diane Baptie.
Parish Registers in the Kirk Session Records of the Church of Scotland, Diane Baptie.
The Parishes, Registers and Registrars of Scotland, SAFHS - contains maps showing the location of parishes, and coverage periods for OPR baptisms, marriages and burials.
Phillimore Atlas and Index of Parish Registers, Cecil R. Humphery-Smith - contains maps showing the location of parishes and commissariots, and starting years for parish registers.
Census Records for Scottish Families at Home and Abroad, Gordon Johnson.

Clans, families and surnames

The Clans, Septs and Regiments of the Scottish Highlands, Frank Adam. First published in 1908.
The Tartans of the Clans and Families of Scotland, Sir Thomas Innes of Learney. First published in 1938.
The Highland Clans, Sir Iain Moncreiffe of that Ilk. First published in 1967.
Burke's Landed Gentry: The Kingdom in Scotland, edited by Peter Beauclerk-Dewar.
Scottish Clan & Family Encyclopedia, George Way of Plean and Romilly Squire.
Scottish Family Histories, Joan P.S. Ferguson - lists the many books published on specific clans and families.
The Surnames of Scotland, George F. Black.
Scottish Surnames and Families, Donald Whyte.
Scottish Clan and Family Names, Roddy Martine.
Scots Kith and Kin.

Other useful Scottish publications

Collins Encyclopaedia of Scotland, edited by John and Julia Keay.
Directory of Scottish Newspapers, Joan P.S. Ferguson.
Scotland's Shifting Population 1770-1850, D.F. MacDonald.
Parish Life in Eighteenth-Century Scotland: A Review of the Old Statistical Account, Maisie Steven.
The Celtic Place-Names of Scotland, W.J. Watson.
Castles of the Clans, Martin Coventry - the history and houses of 750 families.
Scotland of Old (map), Sir Iain Moncreiffe of that Ilk and Don Pottinger - showing where the Highland clans and Lowland and Border families held land at the end of the 16th century.

Scots Heraldry, Sir Thomas Innes of Learney. First published in 1934.
The Queen's Scotland, edited by Theo Lang - a series of eight volumes on the counties and parishes of Scotland (the Scottish equivalent of Arthur Mee's *The King's England* series).

INDEX

FHS = Family History Society

About the SOCIETY OF GENEALOGISTS

Founded in 1911 the Society of Genealogists (SoG) is Britain's premier family history organisation. The Society maintains a splendid genealogical library and education centre in Clerkenwell.

The Society's collections are particularly valuable for research before the start of civil registration of births marriages and deaths in 1837 but there is plenty for the beginner too. Anyone starting their family history can use the online census indexes or look for entries in birth, death and marriage online indexes in the free open community access area.

The Library contains Britain's largest collection of parish register copies, indexes and transcripts and many nonconformist registers. Most cover the period from the sixteenth century to 1837. Along with registers, the library holds local histories, copies of churchyard gravestone inscriptions, poll books, trade directories, census indexes and a wealth of information about the parishes where our ancestors lived.

Unique indexes include Boyd's Marriage Index with more than 7 million names compiled from 4300 churches between 1538-1837 and the Bernau Index with references to 4.5 million names in Chancery and other court proceedings. Also available are indexes of wills and marriage licences, and of apprentices and masters (1710-1774). Over the years the Society has rescued and made available records discarded by government departments and institutions but of great interest to family historians. These include records from the Bank of England, Trinity House and information on teachers and civil servants.

Boyd's and other unique databases are published on line on **www.findmypast.com** and on the Society's own website **www.sog.org.uk**. There is free access to these and many other genealogical sites within the Library's Internet suite.

The Society is the ideal place to discover if a family history has already been researched with its huge collection of unique manuscript notes, extensive collections of past research and printed and unpublished family histories. If you expect to be carrying out family history research in the British Isles then membership is very worthwhile although non-members can use the library for a small search fee.

The Society of Genealogists is an educational charity. It holds study days, lectures, tutorials and evening classes and speakers from the Society regularly speak to groups around the country. The SoG runs workshops demonstrating computer programs of use to family historians. A diary of events and booking forms are available from the Society on 020 7553 3290 or on the website **www.sog.org.uk** .

Members enjoy free access to the Library, certain borrowing rights, free copies of the quarterly *Genealogists' Magazine* and various discounts of publications, courses, postal searches along with free access to data on the members' area of our website.

More details about the Society can be found on its extensive website at **www.sog.org.uk**

For a free Membership Pack contact the Society at:

14 Charterhouse Buildings,
Goswell Road,
London EC1M 7BA.
Telephone: 020 7553 3291
Fax: 020 7250 1800

The Society is always happy to help with enquiries and the following contacts may be of assistance.

Library & shop hours:

Monday	Closed
Tuesday	10am - 6pm
Wednesday	10am - 6pm
Thursday	10am - 8pm
Friday	Closed
Saturday	10am - 6pm
Sunday	Closed

Contacts:

Membership
Tel: 020 7553 3291
Email: membership@sog.org.uk

Lectures & courses
Tel: 020 7553 3290
Email: events@sog.org.uk

Family history advice line
Tel: 020 7490 8911
See website for availability